SAN ANTONIO UNCOVERED

San Antonio

UNCOVERED

Fun Facts and Hidden Histories

Mark Louis Rybczyk

Foreword by Robert Rivard

Maverick Books | Trinity University Press
San Antonio, Texas

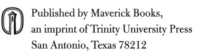 Published by Maverick Books,
an imprint of Trinity University Press
San Antonio, Texas 78212

Book design by Anne Richmond Boston

Image credits: San Antonio Light Collection, Institute of Texan Cultures, San
Antonio Texas, pages 2, 49, 70, 83, 101 bottom, 116 bottom; Nayeli Perez, pages 11,
13, 99 top and bottom, 101 top, 147, 178, 190 top and bottom; Institute of Texan
Cultures, San Antonio, Texas, pages 31, 49 top and bottom, 137, 158; University
of Texas at Dallas, page 58; Prints & Photographs Division, Library of Congress,
HABS, TX-3173, page 112; Zintgraff Collection, Institute of Texan Cultures, San
Antonio, Texas, pages 116 top and 145

ISBN-13 978-1-59534-757-2 paper
ISBN-13 978-1-59534-758-9 ebook

Trinity University Press strives to produce its books using methods and materials
in an environmentally sensitive manner. We favor working with manufacturers that
practice sustainable management of all natural resources, produce paper using
recycled stock, and manage forests with the best possible practices for people,
biodiversity, and sustainability. The press is a member of the Green Press Initiative, a
nonprofit program dedicated to supporting publishers in their efforts to reduce their
impacts on endangered forests, climate change, and forest-dependent communities.

The paper used in this publication meets the minimum requirements of the
American National Standard for Information Sciences—Permanence of Paper for
Printed Library Materials, ANSI 39.48–1992.

CIP data on file at the Library of Congress

20 19 18 17 16 | 5 4 3 2 1

CONTENTS

FOREWORD | Robert Rivard

If you'd like to introduce a newcomer to San Antonio and its rich history or help a friend or neighbor develop a deeper love and appreciation for the city, give them the newest edition of *San Antonio Uncovered*.

I've been privileged to hold a front-row seat on this city's evolution and development for nearly three decades, first as an editor at the now-defunct *San Antonio Light*, then as the longtime executive editor of the *San Antonio Express-News*, and for the last three years, as the founder of the online hyperlocal media site *Rivard Report*. The pace of change is accelerating in San Antonio, and the percentage of the population new to the city is climbing each year. That makes the city's history, heritage, people, and places all the more important to preserve and to share.

The original edition of *San Antonio Uncovered* was published in 1992 by author Mark Rybczyk. It was an immediate hit in a city that cherishes its history. That first edition is on my bookshelf, as is the updated edition published in 2000. Now comes a third edition of the essential armchair guide to San Antonio—its history, unique places, and quirky secrets. Given the city's extraordinary growth and change, this newest edition is most welcome. It's my honor and pleasure to introduce it to you.

When *San Antonio Uncovered* was last issued, the Museum and Mission Reach of the San Antonio River had hardly hit the drawing board. The Tobin Center for the Performing Arts was still the Municipal Auditorium, dark and empty most days and nights. Thoughts of redeveloping HemisFair, expanding the Henry B. Gonzalez Convention Center, and updating the Alamodome for its twenty-fifth anniversary weren't even being discussed.

Southtown was still in its early stages of redevelopment, and Broadway was lined with fast-food outlets and former automobile dealerships. The Pearl was an abandoned brewery. Brackenridge Park's transformation was just an idea. Make a list of the city's top twenty-five restaurants. Most had not yet opened when the last edition was published. The Decade of Downtown was, well, nearly a decade away. Farther out, Hardberger Park, the Shops at la Cantera, and many of the newer buildings on the UTSA campus didn't exist. Neither did Texas A&M University–San Antonio on the city's south side. Brooks City Base was still an air force base. Port San Antonio still looked like Kelly AFB closed.

Reading each edition of *San Antonio Uncovered* is like opening another time capsule and finding a fresh harvest of new stories, some forgotten, some updated. Even natives and lifelong residents will learn things they somehow never knew.

Red McCombs—the billionaire auto magnate, rancher, and businessman—was responsible as a young man for recruiting corporate sponsors for HemisFair '68? Yes.

There is a still-standing aqueduct near Mission Espada? Yes.

The city's Polish and German communities were once so lively they each had newspapers in their own languages? Yes.

The well-preserved Spanish Governor's Palace, half hidden in the shadow of City Hall, once housed a Chinese immigrant mission? And a Chinese-language school once operated nearby? Yes and yes.

No place in San Antonio has more interesting nineteenth-century history than Fort Sam Houston, which sadly remains closed to the general public. With proper photo ID, however, members of the public can still enter the base under certain conditions. (See the Fort Sam Houston website for visitor information.) And one can take in the vast parade grounds where General John J. "Blackjack" Pershing dismounted the horse cavalry in World War I and incorporated mechanized vehicles.

The historic Quadrangle is still roamed by white-tailed deer and peacocks, and one of the state's most glorious Spanish oak trees still offers shade as it did when Geronimo, the famous Apache warrior, was held prisoner there.

Take a leisurely walk in downtown San Antonio, with *San Antonio Uncovered* in hand, and challenge yourself to visit all of the city's early places of importance that still stand today. You will soon realize that visiting all the sites in a single day is simply impossible. You'll just have to come back.

San Antonio Uncovered is like no other book about the city, which has been the subject of so many volumes. It is a thorough and comprehensive compendium that covers 300 years of history, yes, but it's also highly entertaining, quirky, and filled with surprises, anecdotes, and amusing trivia. Never boring, its fun-size bites of information make it easily digestible and suitable for all ages, from schoolchildren to old-timers.

San Antonio Uncovered is atop the stack of bedside books in our home's guest room. With this new edition, we will no longer have to tell visitors about the city's many new attractions, such as the Museum and Mission Reaches and the Pearl, not covered in the last edition. We are good for another decade.

INTRODUCTION

It has often been said that much of history falls through the cracks. If that is true, then *San Antonio Uncovered* is historical caulking. When you thumb through this book, you will notice that the missions and the Battle of the Alamo are rarely mentioned. Many fine books have been written about those subjects, and I have chosen not to duplicate those efforts. I prefer to concentrate on San Antonio's lesser-known history and stories off the beaten track, such as the one about the Travis Club Cigar or the how the World's Largest Boots ended up here. Separately, these stories mean very little; yet, when woven together, they help explain the complex fabric of life in San Antonio.

Any person who has lived in San Antonio for some time possesses a wealth of stories about the city. This book is a collection of those tales.

Who is this book for? It is for the lifelong resident of San Antonio who feels a strange sense of pride when visiting the Pearl. It is for the nostalgic miniature golf enthusiast, who was thrilled when Cool Crest reopened. It is for anyone who has lived here for decades and didn't know that President Dwight Eisenhower was once football coach at St. Mary's University.

Second, this book was written for the newly arrived San Antonian, the non-native, a Texan by choice. Plopped down among the freeways and subdivisions, newcomers may arrive in San Antonio suburbs and wonder, what is so special about this place? Well, there is nothing special about the fast food restaurants, strip malls, and access roads—these are similar to those in any other Sunbelt boomtown. But there's so much more. I am constantly amazed by the number of San Antonio residents who have visited the Alamo and taken the out-of-town relatives to the River Walk but have never visited San Pedro

Springs Park, never stopped at the Sunken Gardens, or never seen (or even heard of) the old Spanish aqueduct. This book is a crash course in local culture.

And, finally, this book is for the frequent visitor to the Alamo City. Millions flock each year to our humble town, spend a few days visiting the River Walk, Sea World, and the Alamo, and then return home. So often, they miss the point of San Antonio.

I once heard a Dallas resident say that San Antonio is a small town desperately wanting to be a big city. He could not have been further from the truth. San Antonio is a big city (well over a million people) that desperately wants to be a small town. It is a town that sees beauty in the old and fights to save it, even if it is something as seemingly insignificant as an old Humble Oil Station. It's people who appreciate the blending of the old and the new at the Tobin Center and do what they can to save what's left of the Hot Wells Hotel. It is a bicultural city that revels in the differences of its people rather than quarrels over them. This, I believe, is the essence of San Antonio.

Seven Little-Known Facts about the Alamo

Perhaps no building is more symbolic of San Antonio than the Alamo. It is arguably the most historic building in the state. Almost every Texan can recite the legend of the Alamo's defenders, but few know its history after 1836.

1 **The Alamo is not a National Historic Site.**
Most sites of such historical significance (like the missions) are National Historical Parks and under the authority of the Interior Department's National Park Service. But with that designation comes the question of jurisdiction. Control of the Shrine of Texas Liberty has been up for debate for decades. After years of being under the watchful eye of the Daughters of the Republic of Texas, the Alamo is now overseen by the State General Land Office, keeping control with the state and not the federal government. The Alamo is, however, on the National Register of Historic Places and is also part of the San Antonio Missions World Heritage Site.

2 **Control of its ruins was in dispute for several years.**
After the Battle of the Alamo, the site was left as a ruin. Many people came to visit the shrine. Some took its stones as souvenirs; others sold trinkets that were made from pieces of the walls. In 1846 the U.S. Army began using the grounds as a quartermaster depot, but they left the chapel unused. When the army made its first attempt to clear rubble from the site, skeletons were found. By 1849 the City of San Antonio, the army, and the Catholic Church were in a three-way court

An aerial photo of Alamo Plaza from 1931.

battle to control the Alamo. It was not until 1855 that the Texas Supreme Court ruled in favor of the Catholic Church because its claim to the site stemmed from a "presumed grant from the Spanish Crown."

3 The Alamo was almost turned into a German Catholic church.

The Catholic Church never intended the Alamo to become a shrine for Texas heroes. In fact, it planned for it to be a place of worship for German Catholics. However, when St. Joseph's was built, the church's chief interest in the Alamo was as a source of income from the army's rent.

4 The famous parapet was not always part of the Alamo.

The contour of the Alamo's roofline is perhaps the most recognized architectural detail in San Antonio. It appears in various forms in hundreds of designs and logos. Perhaps nothing says "San Antonio" more than the Alamo's parapet atop your letterhead. Few realize that this iconic symbol was not part of the original structure but added by the U.S. Army fourteen years after the Battle of the Alamo. Though the Catholic Church had regained control of the Alamo by this point, the army leased and occupied the site. Between 1850 and 1852 it made improvements to the chapel and added the famous parapet. The skyline was designed by architect John Fries and built by David Russi, the team responsible for the Menger Hotel and 1859 Market House.

5 Samuel Maverick lived there.

A few days before the battle, Samuel Maverick was sent to the convention that declared Texas independence in hopes of garnering reinforcements. Although he missed the battle, Maverick returned and built a home on the northwest corner of former Alamo lands, the site currently occupied by the Gibbs Building, where Houston and Alamo Streets intersect. Maverick's insistence that the Alamo was a mission and not a military fort was a key factor that helped the Catholic Church eventually gain control.

6 The Church raised income by selling off and leasing pieces of the Alamo.

In 1877 Hugo Grenet purchased the convent area (also known as the barracks) for $20,000 from the Catholic Church and opened a two-story shop there. In addition, Grenet leased the chapel and used it for storage. When Grenet died in 1882, Hugo & Schmeltzer Wholesale Grocer bought the store. A year later, Sam Houston's son Temple Houston presented legislation that resulted in the state buying the chapel for $20,000, and its control was given to the City of San Antonio.

7 The vice president's granddaughter, Adina De Zavala, fought to save the convent.

Adina De Zavala, granddaughter of Lorenzo De Zavala (first vice president of the Republic of Texas), led the early fight to regain the convent area but could not raise enough money to purchase it. Enter Clara Driscoll, who bought the land and was recognized as the savior of the Alamo. Management of this land was then bestowed upon the Daughters of the Republic of Texas. Unfortunately, the DRT was divided into two factions: one headed by De Zavala, who wanted to restore the convent area, and one by Driscoll, who did not consider that an original part of the mission. Driscoll's followers eventually gained control, securing their leader's place in history. In spite of her efforts, De Zavala was largely forgotten, but her wish to restore the convent area was eventually fulfilled.

When Clara Driscoll passed away in 1945, her body lay in state in the Alamo chapel for public mourning and was later laid to rest in a city cemetery on the east side. Her tomb is just off Commerce Street in the southwest corner of what was once one of the most neglected cemeteries in the city.

Twelve Things You May Not Know about the River Walk (Paseo del Río)

The River Walk is one of the city's most recognizable landmarks, and since the 1980s it has been the second biggest tourist attraction in Texas, right behind the Alamo. The River Walk generates so much economic power—not to mention civic pride—that almost every city in Texas has tried to copy it or is developing similar plans. Most proposals fail, though, because there is so much more to the River Walk than meets the eye.

1 The River Walk is actually a flood control device.

The San Antonio River was not always an object of affection for the city's downtown merchants, especially on September 9, 1921, when a major flood dumped nine feet of water on Houston Street. The water was up to the second level of the Gunter Hotel and washed out merchants up and down the street. It was the twelfth flood to hit the city since 1819, and city fathers felt the need to implement a flood control plan. The River Walk was an elegant solution to the problem.

2 The first flood control proposal was to pave over the river.

Some engineers proposed cutting a new channel for the river and eliminating its big bend portion. The eliminated portion could be paved over for parking or possibly another thoroughfare. This plan was supported by many on the river because an extra street would give them an additional street storefront. Today, the big bend section of the River Walk is not only the most popular but also generates the most commercial revenue of any portion of the river.

3 It took ten years for the proposal to become reality.

In 1929 a young architect named Robert Hugman developed the idea to transform the riverbanks on the big bend into a park-like area with public access and an area of commerce known as the shops of Aragon and Romula. The idea was years ahead of its time; it was decades before urban renewal projects and festival marketplaces were being proposed. The River Walk would feature shops offering food from around the world. The banks would be clear of litter and debris. Merchants would clean up the backs of their property and cease to use the river as an alley and a dumping ground. Hugman proposed this then-radical idea in 1929.

His plan was nothing more than a vision for six years, until local hotel owner Jack White began to look for a way to attract more tourists to San Antonio. White organized a River Beautification Board to promote the idea of a river walk. In 1938 the group proposed a special downtown tax district that would establish $75,000 for river improvement. It was then that the Works Project Administration became interested in the River Walk as a way of putting Depression-era men back to work. The WPA kicked in $325,000 toward the project. Groundbreaking ceremonies for the project took place March 25, 1939, ten years after Hugman made the proposal.

4 During construction, a virtual historic treasure trove was uncovered.

One of the first things that needed to be done during the construction of the River Walk was the cleaning and deepening of the river channel. During the dredging, workers uncovered wagon wheels, cannonballs, guns, and a host of other items.

5 The River Walk has floodgates.

A bypass channel was constructed to have floodwater flow past the big bend area of the River Walk. Floodgates were also built to cut off the big bend area from the rest of the river channel during high water. The two floodgates are just north of Commerce Street and just north of Villita Street.

6 No two River Walk staircases are alike.

Few people realize the effort involved in Hugman's design. The River Walk sits below street level, and thirty-one stairwells were designed to give the public access to the original section of the River Walk. And each one is unique. The first completed stairwell was made of cedar posts and went from the Crockett Street Bridge to the river's east bank.

7 During construction, more than 11,000 trees and shrubs were planted.

Careful attention was paid to landscaping the River Walk. A large number of small trees and shrubs were stored by local nurseries until they could be replanted. Trees that had their roots uncovered by the dredging were treated with the utmost care. Crutches were built to aid many large trees during the construction, and surgery was performed on many large trees. Over 11,000 trees and shrubs were planted. The construction effort attracted attention from across the country. Celebrated columnist Ernie Pyle visited the site in 1939 and wrote an article, "An American Venice in the Making, San Antonio Is Doing Tricks with Its Winding Downtown River," for the Scripps-Howard newspaper syndicate.

8 The visionary who proposed the River Walk originally got very little credit.

It took two years to build the River Walk, which officially opened in 1941. Unfortunately, Hugman had been fired a year earlier. The young architect got caught in a bureaucratic shuffle over materials being sent to the La Villita construction site rather than to the River Walk. A meeting of the river board released Hugman without benefit of a hearing. Officially, it was announced that the visionary architect was released because he failed to hire a landscape architect and because many of his cost estimates were off base. Hugman was devastated by the dismissal.

The man who was known as the father of the River Walk was given very little credit for his vision until 1978, when he was finally recognized for his contributions. That year, bells were added to the Arneson River Theatre and were dedicated to Hugman. Today, as you stroll the River Walk, you will see Hugman's name displayed above his old office, just under the circular Royalty Coins Building.

9 The River Walk was originally a dismal failure.

The River Walk was anything but an instant success. During World War II there was a shortage of labor to maintain the park-like settings. Many businesses resumed their practice of dumping garbage in the water and using the river as an alley. Vandalism and petty crime became common occurrences. Poor lighting made the River Walk a dangerous place after dark. For many years the army declared the River Walk off-limits to military personnel. One air force colonel who returned to San Antonio in the '80s remarked that when he was a young airman stationed in town, the River Walk was a good place to "get rolled."

The first restaurant to open on the River Bend section was Casa Rio, in 1946, by A. F. Beyer. He was joined on the river level by Robert Hugman, who opened his architect office next to the Commerce Street Bridge. Both were the subject of a few raised eyebrows. Many thought they were crazy to operate on the River Walk. Today, Casa Rio is one of the most popular restaurants on the river.

10 A puppet show did not save the River Walk.

A popular local story is that the San Antonio Conservation Society presented a puppet show, "The Goose with the Golden Eggs," to the city council in order to sway public opinion away from a plan to pave over the downtown riverbed section. However, when the Society commissioned Lewis Fisher to research the history of the organization, he discovered that the puppet show wasn't performed until three years *after* the plan had been rejected, apparently to convince the city to protect the city's cultural and historical heritage.

11 The 1968 World's Fair gave the River Walk its second life.
Before San Antonio hosted HemisFair '68, the city appropriated $500,000 to improve the River Walk. The Chamber of Commerce formed the Paseo Del Rio Association, made up of businesspeople who had a stake in the river. The river was extended east toward the new convention center, the first addition in over twenty years. A first-class hotel, the Hilton Palacio Del Rio, was built on the river and was soon joined by La Mansión del Rio. Thousands of tourists who came to town discovered the River Walk for the first time. Soon more restaurants began to open and other hotels were added. The "Shops of Aragon and Romula" that Robert Hugman once envisioned were finally becoming a reality.

12 It was expanded multiple times.
Originally the River Walk ended just after the Tower Life Building. With the construction of the Hyatt Regency, the Paseo Del Rio was connected to Alamo Plaza via a series of waterfalls. It was also extended south to the King William district. In 1988 the massive shopping complex called Rivercenter Mall was built around an extension of the river.

Eight Things to Look For on the River Walk's Museum Reach Extension

Opened in 2009, the northern extension of the River Walk uncovered some hidden treasures, gave new vistas to old treasures, and added a few new ones. Keep your eyes out for these.

1   Two old breweries

The Museum Reach is named for the extension that goes past the San Antonio Museum of Art. This majestic building started its life as the original Lone Star Brewery. In 1981 the old brewery began its second life as a museum. With the addition of the Museum Reach, the museum added a new entrance on the river. Farther north you'll find the Pearl, a mixed-use entertainment and residential development at the once-vacated Pearl Brewery.

2   The oldest VFW Hall in Texas

VFW Post 76 was formed in 1917 by Veterans of the Spanish American War. The post met at the home of Van Petty, designed by Atlee B. Ayres. In 1946 Petty donated his home to the post. The Victorian-style home once had seventeen rooms, five fireplaces, and two kitchens, as well as stained glass windows on both floors. The post's majestic home was rediscovered by the rest of San Antonio when the meandering river behind the home became part of the River Walk extension.

3   A little piece of HemisFair '68

It's been well documented that the World's Fair was instrumental in rejuvenating the River Walk, so it's fitting that a small piece of the fair be included as a piece of public art on the Museum Reach. Look across from the SAMA for a display of metal alloy panels that were once on exhibit at the Taiwanese Pavilion. After the fair, the panels ended up at the home of Anlin Ku, mostly in her garden, where they spent thirty years exposed to the elements. Before her death, Ku asked art patron Mary Lam to take the panels and find them a new home. Lam donated them to the River Foundation, which redisplayed them for the first time in 2011.

4   *F.I.S.H.* and other artistic displays

Artist Donald Lipski specializes in large-scale pieces of public art. For the Museum Reach, he created *F.I.S.H.*—twenty-five

F.I.S.H., by Donald Lipski, under the I-35 overpass near Camden Street.

sunfish, each one seven feet long, that hang beneath the I-35 overpass. The colorful fiberglass lights up at night. A twenty-sixth fish is on display in the museum.

The Museum Reach features numerous displays of public art. Look for artist Martin Richman's *Shimmer Field* under the Lexington Street Bridge, Stuart Allen's *Hanging Panels* under Brooklyn and Lexington Streets, and Mark Schlesinger's *Under the Over Bridge* under Ninth Street. And listen for Bill Fontana's *Sonic Passage* underneath Jones Avenue.

5 The Maverick tile mural

This tile mural near the Lexington Bridge was originally created in the 1930s by Mexican Arts and Crafts, a nearby San Antonio company. It was in the kitchen of a home that was owned by a friend of former mayor Maury Maverick. Art historian Susan Toomey Frost rescued the mural before the house was demolished in 1998.

6 The Ewing Halsell pedestrian bridge

Originally used to roll beer barrels from one tower of the brewery to the other, this bridge was kept in storage for years and refurbished as a pedestrian bridge near the museum. Two new towers, one on either side of the river, were built to support the 8.6-ton bridge, which now belongs to pedestrians. The bridge is named after the Ewing Halsell Foundation, which underwrote its installation.

7 The Grotto

Created by artist Carlos Cortés, the great-nephew of noted San Antonio artist Dionicio Rodríguez, the three-story creation is located between Camden and Newell Streets. Created in the faux bois style (concrete made to look like petrified wood), the caves feature waterfalls, hidden faces, passageways, staircases, and resting places. It has quickly become one of the favorite spots on the Museum Reach extension.

The San Antonio Museum of Art.

8 The 24-foot tunnel intake

Josephine Street and Highway 281 is the beginning of a three-mile tunnel that diverts floodwater from downtown. Constructed in the 1990s, the $10 million tunnel travels underneath downtown and exits just south of Brackenridge High School.

Six Things to Look For on the River Walk's Mission Reach Extension

Opened in 2013, the Mission Reach extension of the San Antonio River connects downtown to the four historic Spanish missions south of downtown. Unlike the original section of the River Walk, which features restaurants and shops, the extension was designed to highlight the area's natural beauty and restore the river's ecosystem. One of the best ways to experience this section is by bicycle. The Mission Reach can also be enjoyed by kayak, with numerous put-in and take-out points.

The missions were originally built adjacent to the river, but in the 1950s the Army Corps of Engineers straightened and channeled the river for flood control purposes. The Mission Reach aimed to clear the river of concrete left behind during the channelization, to reintroduce native flora, and to reconnect the missions along the river with a variety of trails. Here are a few other sights along the way to enjoy.

1 The King William Extension and the Eagleland Project

Before the Mission Reach segment, the River Walk meanders between the former U.S. arsenal and the King William district. The arsenal is now headquarters to the H-E-B grocery chain. The King William district is a neighborhood composed of restored turn-of-the-century mansions belonging to German merchants.

Just past King William is the Blue Star Arts Complex, a series of industrial buildings converted to artist lofts, shops, restaurants, and apartments. The complex also features the Blue Star Contemporary Art Museum and several galleries. Continue on to the Eagleland Project, named for the Brackenridge High School Eagles, whose campus is by the river.

2 The river tunnel outlet and the abandoned swimming pool

The three-mile flood control tunnel rejoins the river past Brackenridge High School. Just past the outlet is the former home of the Lone Star Brewery. Now abandoned, the brewery is awaiting viable redevelopment plans. If you peer through the chain-link fence you can see the large swimming pool and lake that were once used by brewery employees.

3 Future site of Confluence Park

Just past the Highway 90 overpass is Confluence Park, named for the confluence of the river and San Pedro Creek. The San Antonio River Foundation is raising funds to upgrade the small park into a first-class "destination for learning and recreation, inspiring visitors while teaching environmental science and sustainability."

4 People working out at Concepción Park

Concepción Park on the Mission Reach features an outdoor weight room, with innovative equipment that uses your body weight to give you a complete workout. The park also features an overlook walk to Mission Concepción with historical displays of mission life.

5 Functioning acequias

A series of channels was used to bring water from the river to the missions' farmland. Many of the old acequias still exist on the south side. The Mission Reach also passes near an old

Spanish aqueduct and the Espada Dam, built in 1745 and one of the oldest in the country.

6 **Ruins of the Hot Wells Hotel**
South of VFW Boulevard on the river's east side are the remains of the Hot Wells Hotel, once a renowned resort that attracted the famous and well-to-do from across America.

Seven Ways HemisFair '68 Changed San Antonio Forever

In 1968 San Antonio hosted the World's Fair, dubbed HemisFair '68. HemisFair Park now occupies the fair site, located downtown at the intersection of Alamo Street, Market Street, and Cesar Chavez Boulevard, and marked by the Convention Center and the Tower of the Americas, which were both constructed for the event. The city has discussed numerous proposals for the site over the past fifty years, but one thing cannot be denied: HemisFair forever changed the city itself.

1 **It moved San Antonio into the ranks of America's top cities.**
In 1920 San Antonio was the largest city in Texas. But during the Great Depression, the city hit a prolonged period of stagnant growth. In the 1950s, while the rest of the nation was basking in the glow of postwar expansion, San Antonio slid behind Dallas and Houston in population, and its downtown area in the early 1960s looked much like it had in 1930. The idea behind HemisFair was to kick-start the city's growth and propel the city out of its economic slumber.

Perhaps the most telling story of the city's malaise is told by Red McCombs, who served on the fair's executive committee and was in charge of getting major companies to sponsor and build pavilions for the fair. At least twenty companies needed to commit before the fair could be certified, but his initial efforts resulted in signing only three. According to McCombs, the biggest problem was that "major corporations in 1966 thought of San Antonio as being something maybe like Laredo, or maybe like Abilene." With personal appeals from President Lyndon Johnson, HemisFair was able to secure enough corporate partners to have the fair certified. Today San Antonio has over 1.4 million people, is the country's seventh largest city, and is the second largest city in Texas, according to the 2013 U.S. Census estimates of city population.

2 It saved the River Walk.

In 1960 the River Walk was quite different from what it is today. The beautiful Venice-like attraction that architect Robert Hugman envisioned during the 1930s was built by the WPA, but it became anything but an attraction. Most buildings used the River Walk as an alley for storing trash. Casa Rio was the only restaurant on the river, and most thought the owner was crazy to open there. The River Walk was so rough that the military had made it off limits to its personnel.

Part of the HemisFair plan was to extend the River Walk into the fairground, stopping in front of the Lila Cockrell Theatre and what is now the Convention Center. That extension, along with over 6 million HemisFair visitors, helped remake the image of the River Walk. Today the River Walk is the state's second most popular tourist destination.

3 It made San Antonio into a tourist attraction.

From the start of the Depression until the early 1960s not a single new hotel was built in downtown San Antonio. When the city was awarded the fair, it began an era of hotel construction, including the Hilton Palacio Del Rio. The old downtown campus of St. Mary's University was converted into La Mansión del Rio hotel. Millions streamed into the city to experience the fair and discover San Antonio, making it into a first-class tourist destination. Today San Antonio hosts 7 million visitors annually.

4 It gave the city a modern convention center.

Congressman Henry B. González made sure that federal urban renewal funds used for the fair included permanent buildings that could be used after the fair closed. The HemisFair Exhibit Hall became San Antonio's first modern Convention Center. Attached to the hall was the HemisFair Arena, which later attracted San Antonio's first major league team, the Spurs.

The Convention Center has expanded many times, and the arena has been replaced by more meeting space, but the HemisFair's theater remains, now named the Lila Cockrell Theatre, after the city's first woman mayor. If you look above the theater's west facade, you can see an original HemisFair mural, *Confluence of Civilizations in the Americas* by Mexican artist Juan O'Gorman. Today the Convention Center is one of the country's fifteen largest, hosting 300 events a year with over 750,000 annual delegates.

5 It transformed San Antonio's skyline.

By far the most recognizable structure in the city's skyline is the Tower of the Americas. Designed by O'Neil Ford and Boone Powell, the tower was the fair's centerpiece. The top house was built on the ground and raised on to the shaft. The raising of the top house to its final resting stop became a bit of a civic event. The observation deck and the revolving restaurant are still popular San Antonio attractions. Sadly, after the tower was opened and became the city's tallest structure, the observation deck atop the 1929 Tower Life Building closed to the public. At 750 feet, the Tower of the Americas is still the tallest structure in San Antonio, 145 feet taller than Seattle's Space Needle and 187 feet taller than Dallas's Reunion Tower.

6 It changed the political landscape.

In the 1960s the city was run mainly by white businessmen. But the World's Fair opened the doors of political opportunity. Having listened to the community's ideas, city leaders knew it would be disastrous to invite people to San Antonio from all over the world—a myriad of ethnicities—only to have them denied entrance to restaurants and hotels. So they did what they could to make San Antonio an open city to ensure all visitors would be welcome. It was one of the few places in the country to escape the violence of 1968.

7 It wiped a Polish neighborhood off the map.

HemisFair '68 was built on ninety-two acres that were home to one of San Antonio's oldest neighborhoods. The demolition of over 100 buildings, including St. Michael's Church, the country's third oldest Polish Catholic church, was not without controversy. The San Antonio Conservation Society submitted a proposal to save 129 historic structures, some dating back to the 1800s, and have them incorporated into the fair. In the end, only 24 structures were saved, many of which are still in the park. Today there is talk of redeveloping the HemisFair site to include apartments and town homes, recreating the downtown neighborhood.

Seven Lasting Influences of the Spanish Crown

On June 13, 1691, the San Antonio River was discovered by Spanish explorers. Over 300 years later, the Spanish Crown's influence on the city is still apparent.

1 It gave us the name San Antonio.

The river was named for St. Anthony de Padua because it was discovered on June 13, his feast day. Domingo Terán de los Ríos, governor of the New Philippines (as Texas was called then), and Padre Damián Massanet, senior chaplain, were both with the Spanish expedition party that discovered the river, and both claim in their journals that they are responsible for the name. And of course the city that grew up around that river became San Antonio as well.

In addition, Bexar County got its name from the Spanish governor, Martín de Alarcón, who proclaimed the name of the settlement on the river to be the Royal Presidio of San Antonio de Béxar on May 5, 1718. The presidio was named in honor of both the saint and the duke of Béjar (or Bexar), a brother of the viceroy, who had been killed in Hungary fighting the Turks.

2   It gave us the Alamo.

Originally named Mission San Antonio de Valero, the Alamo moved to its present site in 1724, where it was home to Spanish missionaries and Indian converts. The compound later became a military outpost and was defended by a small but determined group of Texas revolutionaries on March 6, 1836, when they were outnumbered by Santa Anna and his army. The site of this Spanish mission is also called the Shrine of Texas Liberty.

3   San Antonio still has four Spanish missions.

In addition to Mission San Antonio de Valero, four other missions were built in the eighteenth century in what is now San Antonio. Concepción, San José, Espada, and San Juan Capistrano were missions that housed Franciscans who converted the native Coahuiltecans to Catholicism and made them loyal to the Spanish Crown. Today these missions are all active parishes, and some parishioners are able to trace their ancestors to those early days. They belong to the largest collection of intact Spanish colonial missions in the country and are also part of San Antonio Missions National Historical Park. Mission Concepción is essentially in its original condition and is the oldest unreconstructed stone church in the United States.

4 The Spanish built the first public water system in the Americas.

In the early 1700s the same Franciscan priests who established the missions also designed channels, known as acequias, to supply themselves and their fields with water. These acequias were engineering marvels, dropping one inch for every hundred feet in order for the water to flow. Perhaps the most impressive feat was creating an aqueduct to carry water over the Piedras creek bed.

The acequias were still being used throughout the city in the 1800s, when they supplied water to beautiful gardens of nearby homes. Prominent German families built houses along the Acequia Madre. Many of the city's early roads followed the acequias; in fact, Main Avenue downtown was originally known as Acequia Street. They also provided a crude sewer system, which was unfortunately a breeding ground for typhoid and cholera. In the late 1800s George Brackenridge's Water Works Company began supplying water to the city, and most of the acequias dried up and were buried.

Small pieces of the acequia system can still be found downtown. The Alamo grounds feature one. Sections of a restored acequia in HemisFair Park are next to the children's playground and in front of the Justice Center on Main Plaza. Pieces of the Acequia Madre and a dam were recently found in Brackenridge Park. Perhaps the best place to view an active acequia is at Mission San Juan Capistrano on the city's far south side. You can follow it along the river, through the woods, and to the aqueduct. Both the aqueduct and the acequias are National Historic Civil Engineering monuments.

5 The Spanish gave us the aqueduct too.

On the south side of town, the aqueduct (or water bridge) that carries water to Mission Espada was built by Franciscans before the United States was even formed. The country's last remaining Spanish-built functioning aqueduct is perhaps the city's most forgotten historic site, but it is well worth the trip.

To get there by car, take Mission Road south from SW Military Drive past Stinson Field Airport. The road becomes Ashley, but continue to Espada Road and turn right. You should be able to see the aqueduct, which feeds water to the acequia, about 200 yards away. You could follow the acequia to the mission, except that you would be trespassing on private property. But a short drive down Espada Road will get you there.

Another interesting site north of the aqueduct is the Espada dam, which was built between 1731 and 1745 and has withstood many significant floods for more than 200 years. The dam, constructed with goat's milk mixed with the mortar to make it waterproof, is all the more amazing because it is curved the wrong way. To view the dam, turn south on Mission Parkway just off SW Military Drive.

6 It designated the city's first park.

In 1729 King Philip V of Spain, via his viceroy in Mexico, declared the grounds at the headwaters of the San Pedro Springs an *ejido*, or public land. The San Antonio Parks Department claims that San Pedro Springs Park is the second oldest park in the country (behind the Boston Commons). It sits across from San Antonio College on San Pedro Avenue and is home to San Pedro Springs Pool and the McFarlin Tennis Center.

7 It gave us La Villita.

La Villita, south of the Alamo on the San Antonio River, was originally home to the families of Spanish soldiers in the San Antonio de Béxar Presidio and is the city's oldest neighborhood. The La Villita Historic District was refurbished under the Works Project Administration and is now the site of shops, artisans, restaurants, and numerous festivals.

Solar Illuminations: A Message from God?

George Dawson, docent at the San Antonio Missions National Historical Park, had heard a local legend from a retiring docent concerning Mission Concepción. It took him ten years to verify, but the rumor was true: over 270 years ago, monks devised solar illuminations that have appeared every year to this day.

It started back in the early 1700s, when Franciscan monks built five missions along the San Antonio River, offering the indigenous people of South Texas protection from Indian attacks and disease, although the true mission of these outposts was to convert the native peoples to Catholicism and make them subjects of the Spanish Crown.

The Mexican Revolution in the early 1800s marked the end of the Mission period. During the next hundred years, the churches and surrounding property passed through many hands and fell into disrepair. In the early 1900s the local Catholic diocese regained control of the badly decaying missions. Saving the crumbling chapels in the 1930s was one of the first victories for the San Antonio Conservation Society. Today the four remaining missions are under the watchful eye of the National Park Service, but the years had taken their toll.

The legend Dawson had heard was that light through various windows at Mission Concepción illuminated certain parts of the church on various religious holidays. For ten years Dawson researched and observed. Then at 6:30 p.m., August 15, 2003, on the Feast of the Assumption (held annually to celebrate the assumption of Mary into heaven) Dawson discovered that light from the two west-facing windows met behind the altar to illuminate a painting of Mary. Simultaneously, a lens above the door created a beam of light centering under the church's dome. This phenomenon, called solar illumination, was used to convey the presence of God to Native Americans, as the light was a metaphor for Christ.

Dawson discovered numerous solar illuminations through the years, including three from the south window of Concepción's dome that marked the Feast of the Immaculate Conception on December 8 and the winter solstice two weeks later. A few years after that, on October 4—which is the Feast of St. Francis—a similar illumination was noticed at Mission Espada, when beams of light lit the statue of St. Francis of Assisi (the Franciscans' founder). On March 9, the date of the Feast of St. Frances of Rome, the illumination effect returns to Espada.

It was also an effective tool in the conversion of native people to Christianity. The sun, Dawson says, "was part of their worldview . . . their religion . . . their lifestyle."

In 2015 the missions were designated a UNESCO World Heritage Site, the first UNESCO designation in Texas and only the twenty-second in the United States.

Seven Things You May Not Know about the Missions

1 **Mission San José's Rose Window was not named after a woman named Rosa.**
For decades, tourists and schoolchildren were told the unusually ornate window was carved by noted Spanish sculptor Pedro Huizar for his sweetheart Rosa. A plaque next to the window repeats the myth. The National Park Service debunked this tale after discovering that Huizar arrived in Texas after the window was already carved. The window is recognized as one of the finest examples of Spanish colonial period ornamentation. Copies of the Rose Window have appeared all over America, including the old Joske section of the River Center.

2 **The staircase to the tower and choir loft at Mission San José was made without nails or rope.**
All twenty-five steps were carved from a single live oak log.

3 **Of the four remaining missions, only the chapel at Mission Concepción has not crumbled over time.**
It is still in its original condition and stands as the country's oldest unrestored stone church. It once featured an exterior painted with brightly colored geometric designs that attracted the indigenous people to the compound.

4 **After the 1824 Mexican Revolution, the missions were abandoned.**
Mission Espada was one of the first to return to active status with the arrival of Francis Bouchu, a Catholic priest, in 1858. He helped to rebuild and restore the decaying church. Later he helped to save Mission San Juan Capistrano to the south.

5 **Benedictine monks from Pennsylvania worked to restore San José in hopes of making it a mission.**
The Brothers of St. Mary, who came to the city in 1859 to establish St. Mary's Institute (later St. Mary's University), were given farmland at Mission Concepción to grow food for their students, and for a time they used the chapel as a barn.

6 **Of all the missions, San José suffered the most decay.**
Its roof and tower are not original. They had collapsed by the 1920s and were rebuilt by the Depression-era Civil Works Administration.

7 **The San Antonio River once connected all the missions.**
The river was channelized in the 1950s for flood control, moving the course away from the missions.

Six Flags over San Antonio

San Antonio was founded under the Spanish flag, and the Spanish influence is still evident today. But the city was and is cosmopolitan, with people from all over the world contributing their cultures.

Mexico

In 1821 Mexico fought to win its independence from Spain. Until the Battle of San Jacinto in 1836, San Antonio was part of Mexico. Though San Antonio became part of the Republic of Texas and later the United States, it has always been a city with a distinct Hispanic flair. Sadly, the Hispanic neighborhoods on the west side often did not share in the prosperity of the young nation. Many of its residents had low-paying jobs, with pecan shelling being a major industry.

When Kelly Field shifted its mission from aviation to logistics, it opened up thousands of higher-paying jobs that propelled many families into the middle class for the first time. Today, Mexican American culture permeates San Antonio, and it is perhaps the most assimilated city in the United States, with some of the nation's first Hispanic mayors, council members, and Congress members.

Experience the culture today: Start your week by attending Sunday mariachi mass at Mission San José. Catch a performance of the Ballet Folklórico or attend one of the city's festivals like the Mariachi Vargas Extravaganza or the Tejano Conjunto Festival. Visit the Guadalupe Cultural Center on the west side, the epicenter of the city's Latino art community.

Germany

Despite its prominent Latino population, historians often look at old San Antonio as a town with a heavy German influence. Approximately 30,000 German immigrants came to South Texas before the Civil War. Books and magazines on Texas were widely circulated on the lower Rhine in Germany, making this portion of North America very popular overseas. Dozens of German villages sprang up throughout the area. Henri Castro established a settlement of Alsatians on the Medina River, which became Castroville. German influences still ring out in New Braunfels, Fredericksburg, and other Hill Country towns.

Immigrant Germans had a profound effect on San Antonio. Most were Roman Catholic and tended to settle southwest of the river along the Acequia Madre in an area that became known as "the Little Rhine." The new residents re-created their European culture in San Antonio. A German-English school located on S. Alamo was founded in 1859. One of the first newspapers in San Antonio was a German language weekly, the *San Antonio Zeitung,* established in 1853.

German businesses and churches began to spring up throughout San Antonio. St. Joseph's Catholic Church and Academy was established in 1867 on Commerce Street. Across from La Villita Street, St. John's Lutheran Church was formed. Menger, Friedrich, Oppenheimer, Groos, Guenther, and Joske are just a few German family names that became associated with prominent local businesses.

Well-to-do German Americans built the King William neighborhood. Named for King Wilhelm I of Prussia, who later became Germany's emperor, the neighborhood was a showplace of stately German homes. The area, built on the old agricultural grounds of the Valero mission, was planned by Ernst Hermann Altgelt (who also founded Comfort, Texas). Many homes had magnificent gardens irrigated with water from the old acequias. The neighborhood was originally planned to cover miles but ended after a few blocks when Carl Hilmar Guenther built his Pioneer Flour Mills. For more than a generation, the King William district, sometimes referred to as Sauerkraut Bend, was the best address in town.

Two events in the early part of the twentieth century provided an end to German culture in San Antonio. The first was World War I and the anti-German hysteria that accompanied it. German was no longer taught in public schools. German publications ceased. For a short time, King William Street was renamed Pershing Avenue.

The second and final nail in the coffin was Prohibition. This caused the end of many German associations, which further eroded the German community. The King William neighborhood lost its appeal as prominent families moved north. Old German families disappeared into the general masses.

Experience the culture today: The King William neighborhood is now a Historic District, with many of the homes restored, or in the process of being restored. Most of these are private residences, but the Steves Homestead at 509 King William Street has been restored to its period elegance and is open for tours. Villa Finale, the only house in Texas that is a National Trust Historic Site, is also open for tours. For information on a walking tour of the neighborhood, contact the San Antonio Conservation Society's office at 107 King William Street. The Guenther House at the Pioneer Flour Mills is now a popular weekend breakfast stop. The King William district is part of the larger Southtown neighborhood, which includes numerous restaurants and galleries, as well as the 1920s era warehouse district that was converted into the Blue Star Arts Complex.

Poland

The first group of Polish settlers came to Texas on December 3, 1854. The Poles who came to Texas were not the stereotypical poor European peasant class; they were farmers, landowners, and taxpayers who lived under the rule of Germans in Prussia. Many Poles left the region to avoid being drafted into the Prussian army and for an opportunity to be more prosperous.

Polish immigration to Texas can also be attributed to the Rev. Leopold Moczygemba. In 1854 the young Franciscan priest was sent to Castroville, where he began to write to his family and friends in his homeland. He realized the advantages the German immigrants had in this new land and believed his countrymen might also benefit from living in Texas.

The first settlers arrived in San Antonio on December 21, 1854. Moczygemba met them in the Alamo City and took them to an area he had chosen for them to start their own settlement. The land was in newly formed Karnes County, where the San Antonio River and Cibolo Creek met. The settlement was named Panna Maria (Polish for "Virgin Mary") and is the oldest Polish settlement in the United States. Some Polish settlers stayed in San Antonio, and others went either to Panna Maria or Bandera (where they welcomed Slavic settlers to help populate their town). In 1855 another settlement was formed on the Martinez watershed that later became St. Hedwig. The original settlers were joined by more Polish families who moved out of San Antonio in the 1870s.

Polish life in San Antonio centered on St. Michael's parish, which blossomed under the leadership of Father Thomas Moczygemba, the nephew of Leopold, who in 1891 became the first Polish Texan to be ordained. The parish and the surrounding Polish neighborhood were destroyed and relocated to make way for HemisFair 1968.

Experience the culture today: Visit the Shrine of Our Lady of Czestochowa (138 Beethoven St.), built in 1966 to commemorate a thousand years of Polish Christianity. To find this somewhat obscure shrine and the Polish nuns who live in the convent there, take the Roland exit off I-10 (east of downtown), travel south to Rigsby, and turn right, then left at Beethoven. If you wish to observe Polish heritage firsthand, look into one of the several active Polish groups that the city still supports, or attend Polish mass at Our Lady of Sorrows Church at the corner of St. Mary's Street and Mistletoe Avenue.

Ireland

Although San Antonio is known for its Hispanic and German heritage, the city once had a thriving Irish neighborhood, originally settled in the 1820s by some eight to ten families who moved from San Patricio (which is Spanish for "St. Patrick"), where they had quite a few problems with Indians. Others came to San Antonio as teamsters or settlers. The area where they resettled was dubbed Irish Flats. Avenue C (now Broadway) was the western boundary, Sixth Street was the northern edge, Bowie was the eastern boundary, and Commerce Street marked off the southern edge. In the late 1800s this was a remote area of San Antonio. The southwest corner of Irish Flats was marked by the John Stevens homestead. Stevens was regarded as one of the leading figures of the Irish community. His home was razed in 1920 to make way for a new post office, the same site as the current post office on Alamo Plaza.

The homes in Irish Flats were unique, combining Spanish, German, and Irish influences. The neighborhood was famous for its parties, wakes, and brawls. It was regarded as one of the liveliest sections of San Antonio, with many festivities lasting until dawn. The Irish of San Antonio worshiped at St. Mary's Catholic Church, the city's first Catholic church to accommodate English-speaking Catholics.

Experience the culture today: Only a handful of homes in the Irish Flats neighborhood still exist, as most have been torn down to accommodate a growing downtown. Each year on St. Patrick's Day, the Harp and Shamrock Society of Texas, dedicated to the preservation of Irish culture and the remaining old neighborhood, hosts a downtown parade and an Irish Festival.

Italy

San Antonio once sported an active Italian neighborhood on the northwest side of downtown, but most of it is now gone, removed by highway construction and urban renewal.

Italian immigrants started to come to Texas in the 1870s, settling mainly in Galveston, Houston, San Antonio, Victoria

Beethoven Hall, before its facade was removed during the widening of Alamo Street.

County, and Thurber County. As with other immigrant groups, word of mouth from a trusted friend was the first impetus to move. Antonio Bruni, an Italian grocer and businessman who found success in Laredo and later San Antonio, convinced many Italians to come to Texas. In 1890 the Christopher Columbus Italian Society of San Antonio was formed. A combination of a fraternal association and a benevolent society, it loaned money to various families in need, taught English, and provided social activities. From its beginning, Italian was the official language of the organization. The society provided land for an Italian community church, and in 1927 San Francesca di Paola Catholic Church was built.

The city was also home to two Italian language newspapers: *Il Messaggero Italiano,* which operated from 1906 to 1914, and *La Voce Patria,* which operated briefly during 1925.

Experience the culture today: The Christopher Columbus Italian Society has remained strong and has been the cornerstone of the Italian community in San Antonio for over a hundred years. English became its official language in 1946, and the group now accepts some non-Italians. It holds Italian dinners and donates money to many worthwhile projects. The statue of Columbus in the adjacent Columbus Park was donated in 1957.

China

San Antonio never had a Chinatown, but the city's Chinese settlers have a rich history. After the Chinese Exclusion Act of 1882 was passed to reduce the number of Chinese immigrants, many Chinese settled in Mexico, hoping someday to become U.S. citizens. They got a chance to show their allegiance when General Pershing pursued Pancho Villa. Pershing was quite surprised when a community of Spanish-speaking Chinese supplied his troops with food and staples during his campaign in Mexico. When he was ready to return to Fort Sam Houston, Villa swore that he would hang every "Chino" who had assisted the general. Pershing led his aides to safety back in San Antonio and convinced Congress to grant them citizenship. The Chinese were so grateful that many named their children after the general, resulting in combinations such as Black Jack Wong and Pershing Yium. When Pershing died, the greatest outpouring of sympathy at his funeral at Arlington National Cemetery was from San Antonio's Chinese community.

When World War I broke out, many of the Chinese were employed at Fort Sam Houston. After the war they began to rely less on government employment and started setting up their own community structure. A Chinese language school was established in 1928 at 215 San Saba Street—the first in Texas. In the early years, classes were taught from 4:30 to 7:30 p.m. six days a week, for students to attend after public school. A Chinese mission was set up in what was originally the Spanish Governor's Palace. The mission became the Chinese Baptist Church in 1923, the first such church in the South. The church's original offices were located at 509½ Commerce Street but later moved to a new building on Avenue B. Fraternal organizations were also formed, including the Chinese Freemasons and a Chinese Optimist Club.

Experience the culture today: The Chinese Baptist Church moved from the Avenue B location to northwest San Antonio in 1994. A number of Chinese cultural societies run language schools and host cultural events.

Birthplace of the Air Force

Each year, thousands of new recruits enter Lackland Air Force Base to start their basic training. San Antonio is not only the birthplace of many air force careers, it is also the birthplace of the air force itself.

In the early part of the twentieth century, Lieutenant Benjamin Delahauf Foulois was serving at Fort Leavenworth when he suggested that the army consider using flying machines and balloons for military purposes. The suggestion was pretty much ignored until the Wright brothers offered the army one of their wrecked airplanes. The army decided to purchase the plane and sent Foulois to San Antonio's Fort Sam Houston to repair, reassemble, and test it. The young lieutenant was perhaps the most qualified man in the army to serve as its first pilot. He had taken a correspondence course in flying and had flown with Wilbur Wright. He was also only five feet, five inches tall and 135 pounds (a small frame was essential for pilots in the early days of aviation).

It took almost a month for Foulois and his crew to repair the craft and make it airworthy. On March 2, 1910, at Fort Sam Houston's Arthur MacArthur Field (named for Douglas MacArthur's father, who was once the post commander), the Wright Flyer was catapulted into the air. The first military flight lasted seven minutes and reached the speed of fifty miles per hour. Gathered on the outskirts of town to see the flight, a crowd of 300 later grew to thousands by the fourth and final flight of the day.

The fourth flight ended when the biplane's fuel line broke, causing it to drop from the sky, and the crash broke the plane's rudder. That ended the day's flying but was the beginning of aviation in the military.

After his first day of military flight, Foulois suggested two innovations that made flight easier and are still used today. One was to replace the catapult launching system with wheels, for easier takeoffs and landings. The second was a result of the mishap on the fourth flight, when Foulois was tossed around quite a bit. To prevent injury on his next flight, he took a leather strap from a cavalry saddle and fashioned it into the world's first safety belt.

After that triumphant day, Foulois spent the next four months setting world aviation distance and speed records. Tragedy struck on May 10, 1911, when Lieutenant George E. M. Kelly was killed in a flying accident over Fort Sam, which suspended military flights in San Antonio for three years. In 1915 Foulois was sent back to San Antonio to organize the 1st Aero Squadron of the U.S. Army, which was the first to see combat in the Pancho Villa skirmishes in Mexico.

Foulois served in World War I as chief of the air service and retired in 1935 as a major general. He died April 25, 1967, two years before a man walked on the moon.

Seven Facts about the Air Force in San Antonio

1 **San Antonio was once the center of the aviation world.**
Because of its flat terrain and ideal weather conditions (it is said the city has only fifteen unsuitable flying days a year), many early aviators came to San Antonio, including Katherine Stinson and Max Lillie. After Benjamin Delahauf Foulois conducted the first military flight at Fort Sam Houston, planes became a familiar sight in the city's skies. The War Department began to realize how useful aviation could be during wartime and soon was expanding the Signal Corps to include pilots.

2 **The army's first aviators trained in San Antonio.**
In 1917 Brooks Field and Kelly Field were opened to train army aviators. Brooks became home to the army's primary flying school, where instructor pilots were trained in the Gosport system of flying, which allowed instructors to talk through a tube to correct a trainee. From 1919 to 1922 Brooks Field was also home to the army's balloon airship school. On Thanksgiving Day 1929, the first mass parachute drop was performed on the base, opening another aspect to aviation warfare. Kelly Field was established as a school for advanced pilots, and for years it was the army's only base for such training. Some of the pilots who had early military flight training at the two bases include Charles A. Lindbergh, William "Billy" Mitchell, Frank Monroe Hawks, Curtis E. LeMay, Claire Chennault, and Henry "Hap" Harley Arnold.

3   San Antonio had to be creative to keep the Air Force.

By 1926 Brooks and Kelly Fields were no longer able to handle the number of pilots the army wanted to train. The War Department wanted to open a new airfield but wanted the land free of cost. Cities from Shreveport to Dallas offered deals to bring the new military complex to their town. The army wanted to stay in San Antonio, but the city had no land to offer. The solution: the city raised $500,000 and dispatched German-speaking civic leaders to convince German farmers on the county's northeast corner to sell their land. Randolph Field opened in June 1930 and soon became known as the "West Point of the Air." It was the nation's only basic school for military pilots until 1939.

4   The Taj Mahal of Randolph Field is actually a water tower.

Randolph Field's beautifully designed base was the pride of the Air Corps. The large white water tower that dominates the landscape was dubbed Taj Mahal and was dedicated on June 20, 1930.

5   Kelly Field was once the city's largest employer.

Kelly Field's main mission shifted from pilot training to logistics during World War II, which made it, for a time, the largest employer in the city. Hiring thousands of civil servants—many from the city's south and west sides—Kelly Field gave rise to a Hispanic middle class and changed the economic complexion of the city, which is perhaps its most important contribution. Today Kelly Field is known as the civilian Port San Antonio and is host to a variety of civilian and military endeavors.

6   The Cadet Center used to be a bombing range.

In 1942 a former bombing range for Kelly Field pilots became the San Antonio Aviation Cadet Center. Named Lackland Air Force Base in 1948 for Brigadier General Frank Lackland, this facility is the military's most widely known base. Because it is the air force's only cadet training center, it's known as "the Gateway to the Air Force."

7 Dedicating a building on Brooks Air Force Base was JFK's final act as president.

In its final incarnation before the base was decommissioned, Brooks Air Force Base became home to the Aerospace Medical Division and the USAF School of Aerospace Medicine. The second oldest active air force base in the country, it was also the site of President Kennedy's last official act as chief of state when he dedicated the opening of a new medical building there in 1963. The next day he traveled to Dallas.

In honor of President Kennedy's last visit, a honey locust tree from the president's Hyannis Port estate was donated to the city and transplanted near the Espada dam.

The Fort Sam Houston Quadrangle and Geronimo

One of the most unusual places in San Antonio is the Quadrangle. The oldest building at Fort Sam Houston, it is now the headquarters of the Fifth U.S. Army. Deer, ducks, rabbits, and other small animals run free inside the fortress. How did the headquarters for one of the world's most powerful armies become a petting zoo? Nobody seems to know. For years, it was open to the public, but since 9/11, access has been monitored.

Until the Quadrangle was built (between 1876 and 1879), the Fifth Army's officers, troops, and supplies were spread out among a variety of buildings in downtown San Antonio. An arsenal that is now the H-E-B headquarters was one of the few structures the army owned. The Alamo was used as a quartermaster depot, and officers lived in the old Vance House (now the site of the Gunter Hotel). When the army was looking for a permanent site to call its own, the city offered land at the head of Leon Springs. However, the army

Members of Geronimo's tribe incarcerated at Fort Sam Houston's Quadrangle.

rejected this because it was low-lying and therefore susceptible to Indian raids. Most of the good land that had some height advantage was in the hands of private citizens. When the headquarters for the local troops was relocated to Austin, city fathers recognized a need to offer a package of decent land or risk losing the military.

The land on the northeastern part of the city became known as Government Hill. The Quadrangle was built without any outside windows or doors (except for the main gate) to provide protection in case of attack. Two water towers and a clock tower were placed in the compound. The bell inside the clock tower was taken from a gunboat that had been grounded in Galveston Bay. It later hung in the Alamo, when the Fifth Army used it as a depot. The clock was installed in 1882 by Bell and Brothers. Oddly, the plaque commemorating the building of the Quadrangle is placed at the top where nobody can read it. It reads:

San Antonio Quartermaster Depot
Erected by an Act of Congress 1876
In Peace Prepare for War

On September 10, 1886, the Quadrangle had perhaps its most famous visitor, Apache Indian Chief Geronimo. Geronimo had been leading the Indians in Arizona and New Mexico in skirmishes against the U.S. Army. The battles were quite brutal, and many died on both sides. According to post records, a Lieutenant Gatewood convinced Geronimo to surrender. The chief and thirty other Apaches were escorted by Captain H. M. Lawton on a special train from Bowie, Arizona, to San Antonio.

While inside the walls, Geronimo was promised the protection of the U.S. Army. Tents were set up to serve as a shelter during their internment. The braves remained in San Antonio until October 22, when they were taken to Fort Pickens, Florida, and confined to an island ten miles off the coast of Florida. There are many stories connected with the chief's stay. One is that the deer in the Quadrangle were brought in for food for the thirty-one Indians. Another is that the Apaches were taken to the Lone Star Brewery and given a tour, where they sampled the beer.

The Quadrangle has changed substantially since then. Windows were added to the outside, the water towers were removed, and the purpose of the structure was changed. On July 30, 1974, the complex was added to the National Register of Historic Places.

As for the animals, legend has it that Geronimo refused to eat army food, and the wild animals were added for his benefit. But in reality, when the Quadrangle was built, occupying a green space with peacocks and ducks was a popular thing to do. Whatever the reason was for their placement originally, those animals' descendants have continued to populate the Quadrangle for over 100 years.

Thirteen Places of Historic Note on Fort Sam Houston Not Freely Accessible to the Public

For years, the section of New Braunfels Avenue that passed through Fort Sam Houston was open to the public as a major city thoroughfare, and visitors were free to come and go. After 9/11, not only did the avenue close, but unrestricted access to the post ended for the general public. Locked behind its gates are some of San Antonio's (and the country's, for that matter) most historic sites.

1 The Gift Chapel

One of the most interesting buildings in Fort Sam Houston is the post chapel, known better as the Gift Chapel. In 1907 Chaplain Thomas J. Dickson started a drive to raise money for a post chapel. Fort Sam had been without one since it opened in 1879. The church, located on Wilson Street two blocks east of New Braunfels Avenue, was built with $43,724 given to the post by the citizens of San Antonio in 1907. At the time, the army installation had outgrown its frontier image and was becoming more of a bustling army post. The need for a house of worship for the troops prompted the city's generosity. On October 17, 1909, President William Taft dedicated the unfinished chapel. Also present at the dedication was presidential aide Captain Archibald Butt, who later died on the *Titanic*.

Over the years, the church was slowly finished. In 1930, a used pipe organ from an old war department theater was installed. The chapel was completely remodeled in 1931 with light fixtures, a grand piano, a cross, and carpeting. Mamie Eisenhower donated money for a set of chimes in 1971 to commemorate her and her husband's association with the post. Some of the more striking features of the chapel are the flags that circle the main sanctuary, which were added in 1971. The Gift Chapel was entered in the National Register of Historic Places on May 17, 1974, and is one of the fort's five chapels.

2 National Historic Landmark marker

In 1974, the 932 buildings and over 500 acres of Fort Sam Houston were designated a National Historic Landmark and Historic Conservation District. A marker designating the honor is displayed on Stanley Road just east of Reynolds Street.

3 Fort Sam Houston National Cemetery

The final resting place of thousands who served their country, the Fort Sam National Cemetery, has some unusual features. Near the back of the grounds are the graves of German, Japanese, and Italian soldiers from World War II. (The soldiers were POWs at Fort Sam.) Numerous soldiers who fought in the Spanish-American War are also buried in the cemetery. Because of the difficulty in carving tombstones during that era, abbreviations were used on grave markers. Thus thousands of veterans are remembered for serving in the SPAM War.

4 First flight memorial

Situated on the other side of Stanley Road, this memorial commemorates the first military flight made by Lieutenant Benjamin Delahauf Foulois in 1910.

5 First WAAC company historical marker

The first company of the Women's Army Auxiliary Corps was stationed at Fort Sam in 1942. Their barracks were at the corner of Lawton and Patch, indicated today by a historical marker.

6 Camp Wilson

In 1916 National Guard troops were mobilized for border skirmishes with Pancho Villa in an area of the post known as Camp Wilson. A marker on Dickman Road between Reynolds and Allen indicates the site. Another camp, Camp Travis, was built shortly after to mobilize troops for World War I. Over 112,000 troops passed through the camp, which was located east of the intersection of New Braunfels Avenue and Stanley Road. Of the 1,400 buildings that were part of Camp Travis, only 3 remain.

7 2nd Dragoon Stables

On Pine Street just south of Wilson is one of the army's last mounted units. Today the unit mainly performs at military funerals.

8 Pershing House

The commanding general's quarters at 6 Staff Post Road are named after Black Jack Pershing, who resided there in 1917. The home is one of the most striking on the post and perhaps in the entire city. It is located on Pershing Avenue just west of the Quadrangle.

9 Eisenhower quarters

At the corner of Dickman and New Braunfels is the home where Dwight and Mamie Eisenhower lived when he was a general stationed at the post in 1941. In 1916 a young Lieutenant Eisenhower lived in the bachelor officers' quarters (BOQs) at the corner of Grayson and New Braunfels across from the Quadrangle. These buildings have recently been restored.

10 Infantry post

At the end of Grayson Avenue are the grounds of the old infantry post, in service from 1885 to 1906. They include the BOQs at the corner of New Braunfels and Grayson, the old officers' mess across the street, the commander's quarters, and the infantry barracks. The post surrounded a parade field. Most of the area is now occupied by enlisted housing.

11 Stilwell House

The commander's quarters for the old infantry post are named in honor of General Joseph W. "Vinegar Joe" Stilwell, who lived there from 1939 to 1940. Stilwell was commander of the U.S. troops in Burma during World War II.

12 The Pat Memorial

Located on Wilson Avenue on Fort Sam Houston, this memorial was erected in honor of Pat the Horse, who retired after twenty-six years of military service when the 12th Field Artillery Unit was motorized. Pat died in 1953 at the age of forty-six, but his memory lives on.

13 Museums

The Fort Sam Houston Museum was recently relocated to the Quadrangle. The U.S. Army Medical Department Museum there is dedicated to military medical history.

Six Military Leaders Who Spent Time in San Antonio

1 Theodore Roosevelt

Roosevelt was the assistant secretary of the navy when he first thought to form a cavalry regiment of Wild West types to fight the Spaniards in Cuba. These famous Rough Riders ended up being a mix of westerners and Ivy Leaguers. Some of the frontiersmen included Rocky Mountain Bill, Rattlesnake Pete, Lariat Ned, and Bronco George, a man who had already downed five men. The westerners drew less attention than the nattily dressed, refined East Coast college-educated men, who stood out in roughshod San Antonio.

Contrary to popular belief, Roosevelt was not the commanding officer of the Rough Riders. Feeling that he lacked enough military experience, the assistant secretary chose Colonel Leonard Wood, who had seen action in the Indian campaigns, as the head man. Roosevelt became a lieutenant colonel under Wood. Roosevelt arrived on May 15, 1898, and recruited members for his crew from the lobby of the Menger Hotel. The bar at the hotel was the site of many impassioned speeches by the future president. The Menger Bar is still intact and has been renamed the Roosevelt Bar.

The First U.S. Volunteer Cavalry trained on the site of Riverside Golf Course, near the water hazard on the sixteenth hole. On May 30, 1898, the volunteer cavalry left by train for Florida; then they went on to Cuba. The Rough Riders suffered many casualties, due to both war and disease. After three months, the Rough Riders disbanded. Lieutenant Colonel Roosevelt went on to bigger and better endeavors.

2 Dwight D. Eisenhower

The future president first came to Fort Sam Houston in 1915, after graduating from the U.S. Military Academy. Eisenhower's two-year stay in San Antonio would change his life forever. It was here that he met Mamie Doud. The young socialite was from Denver, but she spent her winters in San Antonio with her family. While in town, Mamie attended Mulholland School (which later merged with St. Mary's Hall). Dwight wanted to become a member of the army's Signal Corps, where he could become one of the army's early aviators, but concerns from the Doud family made him rethink his career path. After a whirlwind romance, the two decided to marry. The lieutenant bought a ring for seventy dollars from Hertzberg Jewelers, and the couple soon moved into Eisenhower's cramped two-room bachelor officer's quarters.

The apartment on the corner of Grayson and New Braunfels, which still stands today, was known as Club Eisenhower for the number of parties the young couple hosted for their contemporaries. While in San Antonio, Dwight also spent time coaching the Peacock Military Academy football team in 1915 and the St. Mary's football team in 1916.

Eisenhower returned to San Antonio in 1941. This time he and Mamie lived on the corner of Dickman and New Braunfels in a house that is now known as the Eisenhower Quarters. The newly promoted general came to San Antonio as the new chief of staff for the Third Army. Because of a building shortage on the post, the Third Army occupied the sixth and seventh floors of the Tower Life Building. The general's office occupied the corner of the seventh floor. His stay in San Antonio was short-lived, however; after Pearl Harbor was attacked, General Eisenhower was reassigned.

3 Douglas MacArthur

Douglas MacArthur lived in San Antonio when his father was the commander at Fort Sam Houston. The main parade field at the post is named for his father, Arthur MacArthur. The young MacArthur studied at West Texas Military Academy, across from the army post. (The school eventually merged with the Texas Military Institute and the San Antonio Academy.) MacArthur graduated in 1897 at the top of his class, with a 97.35 average. He was captain of the football team and a champion orator. After a five-year stay in the city, he went to West Point. He was stationed at Fort Sam Houston in 1911 and was a captain of the engineers.

4 John J. "Black Jack" Pershing

The Commanding General's Quarters on Fort Sam are named in honor of John Pershing, who lived there in 1917. Pershing spent time here and on the Mexican border in skirmishes with Pancho Villa. During World War I, Pershing left Fort Sam Houston to command U.S. forces. The charge to take on Villa was originally given to General Frederick Funston (for whom Funston Loop is named). Funston died unexpectedly at a function at the St. Anthony Hotel in 1917. He was given the rare honor of having his body lie in state at the Alamo. His command was handed to Pershing.

5 Robert E. Lee

Stationed in San Antonio in the late 1850s, Lee was commander of the local troops from February to December of 1860, in the days before Fort Sam Houston. The then–lieutenant colonel was a popular member of local society and often frequented the German Casino Club. He was also an instrumental member in the early era of St. Mark's Episcopal Church downtown.

Lee commanded the Department of Texas and was in San Antonio when he decided to commit his allegiances to Virginia in the Civil War. On February 16, 1861, he met with secessionists who told him to either resign his commission and join them or leave for Washington without his belongings. Lee declared that he was loyal to the Union and to Virginia, not to Texas revolutionaries. Lee left Texas without his property and never saw his belongings, or Texas, again.

6 Edward White

San Antonio native Edward Higgins White II, the first American to walk in space, was born on November 14, 1930, while his father was stationed at Fort Sam Houston. White was a member of the Gemini 4 mission and walked in space for twenty-two minutes on June 3, 1965. After the successful mission, the city threw a parade in his honor on June 16. Colonel White was killed January 27, 1967, along with Gus Grissom and Roger Chaffee, when the capsule of Apollo 1 caught on fire.

The Truth about Davy Crockett's Tomb and Twelve Other Facts about the San Fernando Cathedral

San Fernando Cathedral, established in 1728 and located on Main Avenue across from Main Plaza, is the cathedral for the San Antonio Catholic Diocese and has become, in addition to a place of worship, a tourist attraction.

In the front of San Fernando Cathedral is a tomb that supposedly contains the remains of Davy Crockett, James Bowie, William Travis, and other heroes of the Alamo. The controversy that started over a hundred years ago about the tomb's contents have mostly been forgotten, and tourists who visit the cathedral take for granted that this is the final resting place of Davy Crockett.

The controversy started in 1889, when Colonel Juan Seguin wrote a letter stating that fifty years earlier he had taken the remains of the Alamo heroes and had buried them beneath the altar at San Fernando Cathedral. Most people dismissed the letter until almost fifty years later, when on July 28, 1936, workmen were digging a foundation for a new altar and they discovered charred human remains. Excitement grew as church officials realized the importance of the discovery. The remains were exhumed with a variety of witnesses on hand, including writer Frederick C. Chabot; Mayor C. K. Quin; postmaster D. J. Quill; Adina De Zavala, granddaughter of Lorenzo De Zavala; and Leita Small, caretaker of the Alamo. The remains were placed on public display for a year, then entombed on May 11, 1938. To quell the rumors surrounding the findings, the diocese published a now rare book, *The Truth about the Burial of the Remains of the Alamo Heroes.*

Some, however, still question whether Davy Crockett is buried there. Most likely he is not. Santa Anna ordered the cremation of all the bodies left at the Alamo. Mexican and Texan soldiers were most likely buried together. Also, Seguin did not return to the Alamo until after the Battle of San Jacinto, almost a month later. There is an excellent argument that the remains are those of the defenders of the Alamo; nevertheless, it is a bit presumptuous to assume that they are the actual remains of Davy Crockett.

Other interesting facts about San Fernando

1. The cornerstone for the church was placed in 1738, although construction was not started for three years. The church is the oldest cathedral in the United States. The St. Louis Cathedral in New Orleans was opened in 1718, but its current structure was built in 1789.

2. After the missions became secularized in 1794, San Fernando became the warehouse for mission properties. Today the church archives contain priceless records and documents.

3. Alamo defender James Bowie was married there on April 25, 1831, to Miss Ursula de Vermendi. The ceremony was performed by Don Refugio de la Garza.

4. Colonel William Travis, on the days preceding the Battle of the Alamo, used the church's tower as a lookout.

5. The church has, on different occasions, been partially destroyed by war, flood, and fire. It has always been rebuilt.

6. From 1868 until 1890, the cathedral had only one tower, the north tower, giving it a lopsided look.

The city's last streetcar in front of San Fernando Cathedral on its final day of service, April 29, 1933.

7. In 1902 the Claretian Fathers were given their first assignment in the United States at San Fernando. The church was the beginning of all their activities in this country.

8. San Fernando once had its own school on S. Laredo Street. The school was built in 1930, and the gym in 1948. The city took control of the buildings in 1967.

9. In 1970, amid much controversy, the Romanesque towers were removed from the cathedral, which restored San Fernando to its original design. Some felt the removal was a bad idea, claiming it lessened the dramatic impact of the church. Others approved because it fell in line with the historical design of the building.

10. At one time, the dome on the cathedral was an important benchmark for mapmakers. The landmark was considered the center of San Antonio, and all streets would be designated north, south, east, or west by their relationship to the dome. (That has been changed; Commerce and Main are now the indicating streets.) For many years the dome was also the mark from which all distances to San Antonio were measured.

11. The cathedral now connects to the River Walk. In 2008 streets were closed, Main Plaza was redesigned, and a new pedestrian portal was added to the River Walk. The cathedral and Main Plaza have become one of the city's most vibrant gathering spots.

12. The cathedral can be used as a giant screen. In June 2014, French artist Xavier de Richemont began using the cathedral for a spectacular free twenty-four-minute light show. *San Antonio, the Saga* is scheduled to show multiple times a week for a decade.

Six Stories That Could Only Happen in the Alamo City

1 The first Battle of Flowers Parade

Fiesta San Antonio is the city's annual spring celebration. The Battle of Flowers Parade is the oldest Fiesta event and has survived two world wars and a sniper attack. Today's parade, however, is very different from the first Battle of Flowers.

The year was 1891. Benjamin Harrison was president, and he was planning a trip to San Antonio on April 21. He was to make a speech on the anniversary of the Battle of San Jacinto. The people of San Antonio were quite thrilled that the president would be stopping in their city. No other president had ever been to San Antonio. A parade and a "battle of flowers" were arranged in his honor. Unfortunately, it rained hard the day Harrison arrived, and the festivities were postponed until the inclement weather had passed. Three days later the rain was gone, but so was the president.

The parade went on as planned. Floats and bicycles were decorated, and most of San Antonio's society people marched through the streets to Alamo Plaza. At the plaza, the crowd split—half to the east and half to the west—to participate in a flower battle that was patterned after a similar event held in Nice and Cannes, France. The two teams threw flowers at each other in a battle that lasted forty minutes.

As the years passed, the flower battle was phased out, but the parade stayed, and more events were added. In 1900 Fiesta became a weeklong event. Today Fiesta has four parades, over a hundred events, and eleven days of fun and merriment.

2 Chili queens

Before there were fast food restaurants, Pig Stands, or coffee shops, there were chili queens. Originally these women would serve chili and other Tex-Mex fare throughout the day to the cattle drivers, tourists, and city folks who would dine in open-air markets. At night, when the farmers would pack their wares, the chili queens would multiply and be accompanied by lanterns, music, and dancing. Most historians agree that the chili queens became a common sight in San Antonio sometime in the late 1870s, setting up tables and kettles at Military Plaza. In 1888 the city hall was built on that site, and the queens moved their trade to Alamo Plaza and Haymarket Plaza.

It can be argued that chili was unique to San Antonio and to the queens. The meat in the dish was tough and sinewy, much like beef was in the 1880s when cattle roamed free. Such a cut of beef was readily available in a major cattle town like San Antonio and easily affordable. The queens also served other Mexican dishes, which many believe are the forerunners of today's Tex-Mex cuisine.

San Antonio's chili queens had a reputation throughout the West. William Jennings Bryan dined in the open-air market. The 1893 World's Fair in Chicago featured a booth called San Antonio Chili Stand. One problem with the stands was their lack of sanitary standards. Nobody was quite sure of the ingredients. In 1900, a chili-stand operator was put on trial for allegedly using horse meat. Maury Maverick writes in his book *A Maverick American* that many locals believed that pigeons, dogs, and other animals were occasional ingredients.

As shoppers moved from open-air markets to supermarkets, and plazas were converted to parks, the chili queens were slowly forced to smaller parks, side streets, and backyards, where their numbers thinned. In 1943 the remaining queens disappeared when they were forced to obey the same health codes as restaurant operators. Once a year, during Night in Old San Antonio, the chili queens reappear, complete with picnic tables, lanterns, and kettles.

An early Battle of Flowers float; the boy second from left is architect Atlee B. Ayres.

Chili Tables, Alamo Plaza, in front of the Postoffice, San Antonio, Texas, 1

Chili stands in Alamo Plaza, 1908.

3 Finck Cigars and the Travis Club

In the late nineteenth century, cigar making was a popular Texas industry, especially among the Germans. Johann Friedrich Ernst, the father of German immigration in Texas, was himself a cigar maker. Only one cigar maker remains today, the Finck Cigar Company of San Antonio. When H. W. Finck, a second-generation German American, set up shop in San Antonio, the city was already home to eighteen other manufacturers. At the time, most American cities had a handful of cigar manufacturers, most being one-person operations. The Finck family lived upstairs from their business, which later moved to a small factory located west of Martin Street. The Fincks' ability to adapt to a changing industry is one reason the company was able to survive.

In 1910 Finck made a special cigar exclusively for members of the Travis Club. The Travis Club was an elite social club for prominent San Antonians, with a multistoried clubhouse downtown. During World War I, the club opened its doors to servicemen, who made it a popular hangout—so popular, in fact, that there was little room left for the members. After the war, the soldiers left, but the members failed to return, and the club folded. However, the Travis Club cigar lived on. The company was flooded with orders from servicemen who had sampled the smoke during their stay in San Antonio. Thus began the Travis Club brand. As for the beautiful building featured on the box, it has been torn down.

Today the company is still going strong, as is the Travis Club line of cigars, which can be purchased today by the general public. The Fincks, now in their fourth generation of cigar manufacturers, are the last of the original cigar makers in Texas.

4 The invention of the Frito

Any true connoisseur of that fried cornmeal snack treat known simply as the Frito will surely know the legend of its origin. As the story goes, Elmer Doolin, future founder of the Frito-Lay company, was in San Antonio in the early 1930s.

According to Frito-Lay, Elmer Doolin owned an ice cream business in San Antonio that was in the middle of a price war, and he was looking for another investment. One afternoon in September 1932, while waiting for a nickel sandwich at a lunch stop, he noticed a small package that sold for five cents. Inside he found a fried-corn snack treat. He sought out the maker and bought the recipe, nineteen retail accounts, and an old converted hand-operated potato ricer used for making Fritos—all for a hundred dollars. Some sources say that Doolin borrowed the money from his mother, who had to pawn her wedding ring. Doolin manufactured the Fritos at night in his mom's kitchen on Roosevelt Street, producing ten pounds of chips an hour. The young businessman sold the chips from his Ford Model T and earned about two dollars a day. In 1933 the Frito company expanded and moved to Dallas.

The man credited with bringing masa, the cornmeal used in Fritos, to Texas is Bartolo Martinez. Martinez learned to make masa in Yucatán and moved to San Antonio in 1896 to begin marketing in the United States. Martinez built a number of masa mills around San Antonio. The first large-scale plant to grind meal into masa was built in 1903, at 701 Leona. It was listed as a national landmark by the National Register of Historic Places.

Eighty-three years later, San Antonio Development Agency purchased the Martinez mill and factory, which sat in the middle of the Vista Verde South redevelopment area. It was set for restoration when a two-alarm fire struck the old wooden structure at 5:22 p.m. on July 26, 1986. Arson was suspected but never confirmed.

5   The last Humble station

Before there was Exxon, there was Esso. And in Texas there was Humble Oil, with service stations across the state and huge refineries that supplied Texans and motorists around the country. On December 1, 1959, Standard Oil of New

Jersey bought controlling interest in Humble and took over. In 1972 the Humble name was replaced by a new moniker, Exxon. Some of the old Humble stations have been abandoned, and others have been remodeled with a new corporate logo affixed above the station. All the Humble stations but one are gone.

The last Humble station no longer pumps gas, but an interesting mosaic on the side of the building marks it permanently as an outpost for Humble Oil. It sat vacant and windowless for years just off I-10 and S. Alamo. It was too small for redevelopment, and many preservationists feared that it would be lost forever. Recently, a dog care business opened next door and annexed the station, preserving it for future generations.

6 Cornyation

Perhaps the most unusual Fiesta event, Cornyation is an irreverent lampoon of all things San Antonio. It started in 1951 as part of Night in Old San Antonio. The production was staged by the San Antonio Little Theater and performed at the Arneson River Theater. Its irreverence caused its demise in 1964 when the whole affair was deemed too vulgar and not family-friendly. There was an attempt to hold the event in 1965 in a downtown Italian restaurant, but it was so poorly attended that the event died out.

The show was revived in 1979 for one year, then again in 1982, growing from its first performances in the Bonham Exchange ballroom to an annual Fiesta performance at the Empire Theatre. Cornyation now has its own court, featuring King Anchovy, named after the first Cornyation 1951 Court of the Cracked Salad Bowl. Fiesta Cornyation is now a nonprofit organization that has donated over $1.5 million to HIV-related charities and awards scholarships to San Antonio theater majors.

Five Events That Really Did Happen in San Antonio

1 And the first Oscar goes to *Wings*

The first movie to win the Oscar for Best Picture has its roots in the Alamo City. The silent World War I epic *Wings* was filmed in San Antonio, using its many military facilities as backdrops, including cadet training sites, Kelly and Brooks Fields. The Fort Sam Houston gate near the Quadrangle was in the opening shot, and Camp Stanley stood in for Saint-Mihiel, France, where the 2nd Infantry fought.

The film premiered in San Antonio on May 19, 1927, at the Texas Theatre. Proceeds from the event—$5,500—were given to a memorial fund for the 2nd Infantry, which lost 25,000 troops in World War I. Actors Buddy Rogers, Clara Bow, Richard Arlen, and Jobyna Ralston attended the premier of their film, as did many actors from the movie *Rough Riders*, which was filming in San Antonio at the time. The movie also features the screen debut of Gary Cooper, who was on screen for 102 seconds. Cooper received such a reaction from fans who wrote the studio asking about the tall actor that his fate as a star was sealed.

The premiere ended on a spectacular note, when moviego-ers left the theater and were greeted by newsboys who were selling papers announcing that former Brooks Field Cadet Charles Lindbergh was preparing to leave for Paris on his solo transatlantic flight.

2 The San Antonio Blue Book

San Antonio was once a wild frontier town. The last civilized stop before heading west and the largest city in Texas, San Antonio at the turn of the century was a center for vice. From the Civil War until World War II, the city supported one of the most notorious red-light districts in the country. Dubbed

Wings movie poster.

the Sporting District, it was in the southwest end of downtown, bounded by Durango Street on the south, Santa Rosa on the east, Market Street on the north, and Frio on the west. The area is now mainly occupied by the elevated portion of I-35 and the police headquarters.

The district grew into prominence after the Civil War and was frequented by soldiers on leave, East Coast businessmen who were visiting area resorts, cowboys and cattlemen who were passing through the area, ranchers and farmers in town to market their goods, prominent local businessmen and politicians, and citizens from all walks of life.

The area was divided into three types of brothels. Class A brothels were by far the best. Located in fine mansions, many built by the same architects who built the homes in the King William district, these establishments were frequented by well-heeled patrons who stayed for about a week, sharing the company of one lady. These houses offered well-stocked bars, gambling, player pianos, and velvet furniture coverings and drapes, along with brass rails and paintings of nudes. Patrons usually enjoyed some gaming, dancing, and drinks before retiring for the evening.

Class B houses were usually upstairs in a saloon or a second-class hotel. Finally, class C women worked out of "cribs," rundown shacks with small rooms. The women stood outside their small quarters and enticed men on the street. Fees varied depending on the type of establishment. A stop at a class A brothel cost a dollar, class B women charged fifty cents, and class C cribs cost a quarter (thus the derogatory phrase a "two-bit whore"). Visitors learned quickly of the red-light district from cab drivers and police, who were only too anxious to direct tourists to the Sporting District and secure a generous tip for themselves.

Perhaps the most unusual aspect of the brothel industry was *The Blue Book*, a directory of the area's houses that listed cab drivers who would take passengers to the district and listed the ladies and madams who operated in the area. The

1911–12 edition also included the schedule for San Antonio's baseball team and information about the area's cockfights.

During World War II, one frequent visitor said that parents who had heard stories of the wildness of San Antonio (and perhaps had visited the establishments themselves during their earlier days) pressured the army into shutting down the Sporting District. Regardless of the source, the army issued this threat: "Close down the brothels or we will place all of downtown S.A. off-limits to the soldiers." Mayor Charles K. Quin, along with his police commissioner, flushed out the brothels, ran the women out, and put an end to one of the city's most notorious chapters.

3 The alligator in the San Antonio River

San Antonio is not a natural habitat for alligators, so stories of alligator sightings in local waterways are usually dismissed as urban legends. But the San Antonio River has been home to at least one alligator. On November 4, 1989, officials from Texas Parks and Wildlife were alerted to the presence of an alligator near the Espada dam. The next day, game officials searched the river in the morning and again in the afternoon. With the help of local fishermen and a casting net, state game warden Denny Villalobos pulled a three-foot alligator from the water. State officials speculated that either the alligator was dropped into the river by someone who had originally kept the creature as a pet, or it migrated north when its water hole evaporated. A month earlier in Medina Lake, a seven-foot alligator had been found dead with a blow to the head, possibly from a motorboat.

4 Sam, the space monkey

Sam was the first Texan to travel into space. Born in 1957 at the University of Texas, the rhesus monkey was designated for the U.S. space program because he was a standout at the UT Balcones Research Center. On December 4, 1959, in Wallops Island, Virginia, after a seventeen-hour countdown, Sam was launched fifty-five miles into space and spent a total of twelve minutes there. The famous flight earned him the cover of *Parade* magazine in 1960.

Afterward, Sam was brought to the School of Aerospace Medicine at Brooks Air Force Base, where he was put under medical scrutiny for eleven years. Once the air force had gathered enough evidence on the effects of space flight on monkeys, Sam was moved to the San Antonio Zoo, where he was given a companion, though he was too fat to mate. A plaque on his cage told zoogoers of his accomplishments.

The space pioneer passed away on September 19, 1978. An autopsy was performed on him at Brooks to learn more about the effects of weightlessness.

5 The camels arrive

In 1856 the people of San Antonio viewed one of the most unusual sights of their lives—a troop of camels marching through the streets of downtown. Thus began the camel's brief history with the army.

Previously, the army relied heavily on mules to transport supplies, but many in the War Department felt camels would better suit the wide-open spaces of the Southwest. Camels could move faster than mules, and because of their ability to store great amounts of water, their routes were not limited to those that had water. They could travel through mud better than mules and could carry heavier loads with less upkeep and less equipment. So Secretary of War Jefferson Davis sponsored an experiment to use the desert creatures as a pack animal for the army.

In May 1856 thirty-four camels arrived in Indianola, where Brevet Major Henry C. Wayne took charge of their journey to San Antonio. On June 18 they camped briefly at San Pedro Springs to rest and refuel before moving on to Camp Verde, an experimental outpost near Kerrville. Some camels spent the rest of their lives there, some went to circuses, and others were sold to private individuals.

Although the pack animals passed all their tests, they never caught on with the army. Military horses were unruly around the camels, most likely due to their odd appearance or strong odor. But mainly the camels suffered poor public relations. Despite their excellent performance, people disliked them and preferred to stick with the more familiar horse and mule.

Katherine Stinson and the Stinson School of Flying

The early days of aviation were a most exciting time. The few who dared to enter a flying machine were among the era's most popular celebrities. Most of the pilots at that time were men. Few believed that the skies were a place for women. Katherine Stinson thought differently.

Stinson was looking for a way to raise money for a trip to Europe. She had heard that pilots could earn $1,000 a day, an unheard-of amount in 1910. After receiving the skeptical approval of her parents, the nineteen-year-old set out to learn to fly. Finding a flight instructor was a feat in itself because there were only 200 licensed pilots in the world.

Two years later, Stinson sought the help of famous aviator Max Lillie of Chicago, who was not enthusiastic about taking on a female student who was barely five feet tall and just over a hundred pounds. But Stinson proved herself to her instructor. After a mere four hours of lessons, she soloed. She acquired her license in July 1912 from the Federation Aeronautique Internationale, becoming the fourth woman pilot in America.

Onlookers flocked to fairs and open fields to see the "flying schoolgirl." In 1913 Stinson opened the Stinson Aviation Company in Hot Springs, Arkansas, with her mother. A short time later, Max Lillie convinced her family to move to San Antonio, where the mild winters and terrain were perfect for year-round flying. He had convinced the army to let him use the Fort Sam Houston parade ground as a landing strip. Stinson regularly flew over the city, performing stunts. She taught herself the difficult and dangerous loop-the-loop and was the first woman to perform it. It soon became part of her flying repertoire.

Stinson traveled to air shows by train, reassembling her plane at each stop so meticulously that other pilots teased her. Her reputation grew as she continued to tour. In Los Angeles she spelled out the word "Cal" with fireworks, becoming the first pilot to skywrite at night. In London she amazed audiences by flying around the Houses of Parliament and St. Paul's Cathedral. She toured Canada when most people there had never seen a flying machine. In 1916 she traveled to Tokyo, where 25,000 fans turned out to watch her fly. Katherine Stinson fan clubs sprang up all over Japan. She made thirty-two appearances in China, including a private show for Chinese leaders. Her fame had spread worldwide.

When World War I broke out, the U.S. Army asked for pilots to volunteer for service. Stinson offered her talents to the army but was turned down because she was a woman. The aviatrix had to be satisfied with raising money for the Red Cross as her contribution to the war effort.

Stinson moved on to other flying accomplishments. On December 17, 1917, at 7:31 a.m., she left San Diego in a special plane designed to fly at 85 miles an hour and hold enough fuel to get her 700 miles. At 4:41 p.m. she landed in San Francisco with two gallons of fuel left. Her trip of 610 miles set a new world record. She had covered more miles and had been airborne longer than any pilot ever—man or woman.

With her place in aviation history secure, she again applied to the army to be a reconnaissance pilot but was again turned down. She was finally accepted into the military as a volunteer ambulance driver and served in London and France during the war.

As the war drew to a close, Stinson contracted tuberculosis. The treatment was a warm climate and rest. Her flying days were over, and she retired to New Mexico, where she married World War I airman Miguel Otero Jr. in 1928. Stinson died at age eighty-six in Santa Fe, in 1977. San Antonio's Stinson Municipal Airport and Stinson Middle School are both named in her honor.

Eight Incredible San Antonio Characters

1 John "Bet-a-Million" Gates

Until the 1870s cattlemen throughout Texas let their cattle run free across the open plains. Large ranches were nonexistent. Because of the lack of wood and rocks on the Texas plains, ranchers had few materials with which to make fences, making it difficult to protect their property. But a young Illinois native came along and changed all that.

John Warne Gates, twenty-two and just out of college, came to San Antonio to peddle an unusual product—barbed wire, manufactured by the Washburn Moen Company. Gates claimed that the wire was stronger than whiskey and cheaper than dirt, and there wasn't a steer that could get through it. But cowboys were skeptical, and despite the number of cattlemen passing through town on their great trail drives to Kansas City, Gates could not find any customers. So the young salesman convinced city officials to let him construct a corral on Alamo Plaza, where he invited cowboys to bring their longhorns. After they saw how the fence tamed the wildest steer, Gates sold a boxcar full of wire.

That year 3 million pounds of wire were sold. The next year sales more than quadrupled. Eighty million pounds were sold by 1880, and the cattle business was changed forever. The open range disappeared as landowners fenced off their land to protect their watering grounds and cattle. Cattle drives were replaced by trains, which were spreading coast to coast. The longhorn lost out to fine beef cattle. By 1884 cutting a barbed-wire fence was a felony.

As for Gates, he formed his own barbed-wire company and made a fortune. The flamboyant wheeler-dealer picked up the name Bet-a-Million from his gambling exploits and later played a role in the oil boom that hit in 1901.

A historical marker commemorating this unusual demonstration was placed in 1971 near City Hall, mistakenly stating that the event took place on Military Plaza.

2 The Lucchese family

For over a hundred years, the name Lucchese has meant only one thing in San Antonio—the finest-quality boots. The company that has come to be associated with first-class footwear was founded by Salvatore "Sam" Lucchese, a native of Palermo, Italy, who was born in 1866 into a boot-making family. In 1882 he arrived in Galveston and a year later set up shop in San Antonio at the age of seventeen. Shoemaking was a popular business for Italian immigrants because it required little financial outlay to get started.

The large number of army personnel at nearby Fort Sam guaranteed the Lucchese Boot Company an ample supply of customers. The shop on 317 E. Houston made riding boots for graduating cadets in the Army Air Corps until they were discontinued as part of the uniform in 1934. The army followed suit in 1938. Lucchese's boots continue to be popular with the cadet corps at Texas A&M University.

But the Luccheses did just fine without the military because everybody seemed to want a pair of custom-made boots. After World War II, second-generation boot maker Cosimo Lucchese often raised the price of their product to cut back on demand and ensure they would not have to rush. When the demand fell, Cosimo lowered the price again.

Many prominent Texas families and famous Americans have had the Luccheses make their boots. In 1898 the founder crafted a pair for Teddy Roosevelt when he was in town with the Rough Riders. General Henry "Hap" Harley Arnold, head of the U.S. Army Air Corps in World War II, wore Luccheses, as did Generals Eisenhower, MacArthur, and Patton. Also among those measured for a pair of custom-made boots were Gene Autry, Bob Hope, John Wayne, Jimmy Dean,

Gregory Peck, Jimmy Stewart, and Bing Crosby. The boot company stayed in the family for many years, passing from Salvatore Lucchese to son Cosimo to grandson Sam, who made boots for Lyndon Johnson.

Salvatore Lucchese's daughter Josephine made a name for herself outside the family business. With her debut as a coloratura soprano in New York in 1922, she became the first serious opera talent who studied in America. Madame Lucchese became known as "The American Nightingale" in Milan, New York, and other sites around the world. She sang opposite some of the leading tenors of her time, including Tito Schipa and Giovanni Martinelli. For many years she was the leading soprano of the Philadelphia Grand Opera Company. From 1957 until 1970 she was on the music faculty at the University of Texas and continued to give private voice lessons to exceptional students.

3 Samuel A. Maverick

The *American Heritage Dictionary* defines *maverick* as "1. An unbranded or orphaned range animal, especially a calf. 2a. a nonconformist. 2b. An independent as in politics." It lists the origin of the word as "Samuel A. Maverick, Texas cattleman."

Maverick was a signer of the Texas Declaration of Independence, an Alamo defender, and a prominent San Antonian. And, according to Texas legend, he was a cattleman of mammoth proportions, owning mighty ranches and sending thousands of cattle to market every year. Because Maverick's cattle roamed free on the plains, unbranded, cowboys who came across an unbranded cow would exclaim, "That's Maverick's cow." Thus, any unbranded cattle became known as *mavericks*. The term was passed around the West and evolved to mean anybody who was an unbranded or wild character.

However, Samuel's grandson, Maury Maverick, wrote in his book *A Maverick American* that his grandfather was never a cattle baron. In 1845 Samuel Maverick had 400 head of cattle and left them with Jack, a caretaker who never bothered to brand them. The herd was placed on a peninsula, but the water was so shallow that cattle crossed it to the mainland, where Jack let them wander freely. The small herd was finally branded and sold in 1853. The legend of Maverick, the so-called cattle baron, was spread west in 1849 by those who landed on the Texas coast on their way to the California Gold Rush.

Samuel Maverick was surely a heroic Texan, but a cattle baron? That is little more than a Texas tall tale.

4 Father Carmelo Tranchese

Father Carmelo Antonio Tranchese was pastor of Our Lady of Guadalupe and one of the most respected figures on the west side.

Before coming to America, Tranchese held a high position at the University of Naples, teaching physics and literature. He spoke French, Spanish, Italian, English, and Latin. When he came to San Antonio in July 1932, he saw poverty that he had not even imagined was possible in America. Our Lady of Guadalupe served 12,000 desperately poor parishioners, it was deeply in debt, the building was in disrepair, and the parish house had only apple crates for chairs. The west side neighborhood around it was one of the worst slums in the United States. The death rate was three times the national average.

After the Fair Labor Standards Act of 1938 established a minimum wage of twenty-five cents an hour, a bad situation got worse. Most of the west side workers were pecan shellers who worked for the ridiculously low wage of $1.50 a week. Instead of receiving raises, the shellers were dismissed from their jobs and replaced with machines. Father Tranchese worked with San Antonio mayor Charles K. Quin to collect food for over 8,000 desperate residents.

The priest was also appalled by the lack of decent housing for the people of his parish. Most lived in small shacks without adequate plumbing. Father Tranchese convinced the Junior Chamber of Commerce to purchase the property and demolish the shacks, so that adequate housing could be built. Unfortunately, the old structures were torn down, but nothing was built to replace them.

Tranchese worked with U.S. Congressman Maury Maverick to get the federal government to build affordable housing on the west side, but there were many obstacles. The Supreme Court challenged the constitutionality of public housing, and numerous threats were made on Tranchese's life, but the priest was finally able to convince the U.S. Housing Authority to build the Alazán-Apache Courts in 1939, the city's first public housing project. The project had to be scaled back because landowners charged exorbitant prices for the property. Still, the new apartments were a vast improvement for those lucky enough to get them. Rents ranged from $8.75 to $11.25 a month, depending on apartment size, which was comparable to the rents charged to those living in the shanties.

Tranchese also worked to establish a child health clinic, a nursery school, and a playground, and he helped form a class where young girls could learn their native dances. He retired in 1953 to Louisiana and died three years later. To the people of the west side, he is remembered as El Padrecito, one of the first people who worked to improve the quality of their lives.

5 Emma Tenayuca and Maury Maverick

The American South was never a bastion of communism. During the 1930s it was a new concept embraced by many labor leaders and liberal intellectuals. But in the South, where even labor unions were frowned upon, the communist movement never gained traction.

The exception was San Antonio. With its large population of Mexican Americans who lived in poverty, the city proved to be a fertile ground for communist agitators. Many of the Latinos in San Antonio were the pecan shellers who lost their jobs when the minimum wage went into effect in 1939.

Emma Tenayuca leading a workers' rally on the steps of City Hall.

Emma Tenayuca, a union activist married to Homer Brooks, was appalled by the poverty on the west side. Standing only 5 feet 1.5 inches tall, she grew up in comparatively comfortable conditions. By the time she graduated from Brackenridge High School, she had denounced the Catholic Church and become a communist. In 1932 she began organizing strikes and soon took over the local chapter of the Worker's Alliance. Throughout the west side, she was known as La Pasionaria after the communist passion flower of the Spanish Civil War. For her efforts, she was arrested twice, and her local headquarters were often trashed by the police. Her followers once took over City Hall, and on another occasion they organized a sit-down at the police station. Despite all that, few took her seriously, and she was mostly considered a nuisance.

In August 1939, in an effort to impress her East Coast contemporaries, Tenayuca wrote a two-sentence letter to the mayor requesting the use of the Municipal Auditorium for a communist rally. Mayor Maury Maverick—a staunch defender of the Bill of Rights, an attorney for the American Civil Liberties Union, and a former New Deal congressman— granted a permit for the rally, knowing full well that he might also be signing away his political career.

A week before the gathering, it was revealed that Russia had signed a nonaggression pact with Nazi Germany. Americans believed they would soon be pulled into World War II, and Russia's actions caused anticommunist sentiment to swell. The rally's timing could not have been worse. Church and veteran groups protested the permit, but the mayor refused to revoke it. Many were appalled that the Municipal Auditorium, which was dedicated to those who served in World War I, would be used by communists.

On the day of the rally, a poster of Joseph Stalin was hung inside the hall. The mayor believed that the meeting would take place without incident, but he had most of the police on hand just in case. His prudence proved to be justified. Despite the fact that only 100 people showed up for the rally, 5,000 showed up to protest. The mayor could hear the angry crowd from his home two miles away.

The mob threw stones and burned Maverick in effigy. Ignoring tear gas and water hoses, they rushed the auditorium. Tenayuca and her followers escaped with police escorts via the basement. When the horde entered the auditorium, they proceeded to break every window in the place and slash all the seats. Fire hoses were cut, and the rioters held their own victory rally inside. Fourteen police officers and a host of protesters were injured in the melee.

The events of August 25 had many aftereffects. Emma Tenayuca, the young, petite communist leader, was never heard from again. As for the city of San Antonio, it had suffered its most disgraceful moment, with the eyes of the nation watching. Conservative and liberal newspapers alike condemned the mob action, and one national magazine, the *Forum and Century,* labeled San Antonio "the Shame of Texas."

As for Maury Maverick, his career as mayor would soon be over. His many accomplishments (such as the restoration of La Villita) and his years in the U.S. Congress meant little to the electorate who dumped him the next year. For a long time he was remembered simply as "the guy who let the commies use the auditorium."

A popular story that circulated throughout the city afterward had Maverick leaving a church service when a prominent woman cornered him and said, "What are you doing in church? I heard talk all over town you're a communist, but I guess you couldn't be if you go to the Episcopal Church." He replied, "I hear all over town that you're an old whore, but I guess you couldn't be if you go the Episcopal Church."

6 Aureliano Urrutia

Thousands of people each day drive by a small park on Hildebrand near Broadway, next to the AT&T building. On the park's ornate gates is the name Urrutia in tile. Who was Urrutia, and why all the sculptures?

The park was originally the summer home of Dr. Aureliano Urrutia, a famed surgeon who liked the area near the San Antonio River's headwaters because it reminded him of his native Mexico. Urrutia gained notoriety at the turn of the century, when he was the personal physician of President Porfirio Díaz. In 1913 the doctor was appointed Minister of the Interior during the dictatorship of Victoriano Huerta. It was rumored that Urrutia was a henchman for Huerta and that he had cut out the tongue of an opposition leader. Urrutia also sent an ultimatum to Woodrow Wilson demanding that he recognize the Mexican government as legitimate. Wilson sent the marines.

Urrutia went into exile because of the Mexican Revolution and eventually settled in San Antonio. Soon after moving to San Antonio, he gained worldwide recognition when he separated a pair of conjoined twins in 1917. Urrutia built a beautiful mansion on Broadway and dubbed it Quinta Urrutia. This castle-like home, with its beautiful gardens, sculptures, and fountains, was a showplace and gathering spot for the social elite in the 1920s. The doctor opened a clinic downtown and built a summer home dubbed Miraflores on the northern edge of town.

Another fantastic story about the doctor allegedly occurred at a party in the St. Anthony Hotel, where General Frederick Funston was also a guest. Funston and Urrutia had a few confrontations during the tumultuous days of the Mexican Revolution, and there was no love lost between the two. According to the legend, Urrutia flashed the general "the evil eye," and Funston fell over and died. (Funston did indeed die at the St. Anthony Hotel during a social event on February 19, 1917. As the band began to play "Blue Danube," Funston collapsed and died of heart failure.)

Despite the persistent rumors, Urrutia was a great doctor. He performed 6,000 operations before retiring at age eighty-eight in 1959. He fathered eighteen children, many of whom became doctors and served with their father. In 1962 he sold Miraflores to USAA Insurance for $300,000. (USAA later sold the park and its headquarters to Southwestern Bell.)

Quinta Urrutia was sold a short time later and eventually became home to a car dealership located at 3225 Broadway.

Urrutia, who was famous for always wearing an opera cape, died in 1975 at the age of 104. The land on Hildebrand has been ceded to the city and is scheduled to become part of Brackenridge Park. The archway entrance was moved to the San Antonio Museum of Art in the 1990s, where it was restored and is on display.

7 O. P. Schnabel

Every time you turn a San Antonio street corner and see a trash receptacle, you can thank O. P. Schnabel. When you notice area merchants cleaning up outside their businesses next to a Beautify San Antonio award, you can thank him again. What began as one man's forty-year campaign to keep litter off the streets blossomed into a citywide effort to beautify San Antonio. It all started with the man known simply as Mr. Clean.

Schnabel started working at Jefferson Standard Life Insurance Company in 1919. A successful insurance salesman, he rewarded himself in 1947 with a trip to Switzerland. He was inspired by the cleanliness of the European cities, and he returned home with a goal to stamp out litter locally. While many people talk of making a change, Schnabel put his plan into action. He founded the Beautify San Antonio Association and started one of the first antilitter campaigns in America. He helped the city acquire trash receptacles for street corners, and his organization offered awards to area merchants who beautified their grounds. He went on to found the Beautify Texas Council and was often seen picking up trash on the streets of downtown.

San Antonians jested that O.P. (born Otto Phillip Schnabel) stood for Old Pushbroom. The city honored the antilitter pioneer by naming a park after him on the northwest side.

Schnabel's trademark was a shiny new penny glued to a business card wishing people good luck and asking them not to litter. He started giving away pennies in 1926, and he once estimated that he had handed out $70,000, one penny at a time.

8 Bongo Joe

Anyone who frequented the River Walk in the 1970s and '80s surely will recall an enigmatic street musician known as Bongo Joe. For almost twenty years, Bongo Joe would tow his crude sound system with his moped to the traffic triangle in front of the Chamber of Commerce office and beat out music throughout the evening. Drumsticks made with many layers of tape and two fifty-five-gallon drums were all Bongo Joe needed to entertain downtown revelers with song. A "God-given gap" between his teeth, Joe claimed, gave him the ability to whistle perfectly.

George "Bongo Joe" Coleman was born in a Florida orphanage sometime in the 1920s (he was infamous for giving a variety of birth dates). After a stint in the U.S. Army he landed in Galveston but came to San Antonio for the 1968 World's Fair. Soon after the fair ended he began drumming on the street, and his nightly performances quickly became a downtown institution. Word of the drumming street performer spread across Texas. Gary P. Nunn mentioned Bongo Joe in his song "What I Like about Texas." A California recording company made an album of his music.

Sadly, the 1980s were difficult years for Bongo Joe. In 1982 his moped was stolen. Later that year the Museum Association wanted to demolish his $45-a-month flat. In 1983 he was involved in a fracas with a heckler that ended in a shooting, for which he was sentenced to five years of probation. The year 1986 found Bongo Joe once again facing eviction from developers. By the end of the decade, the street performer had stopped coming downtown.

It seemed as if he had disappeared. An Austin weekly even printed a eulogy for him. But after a month-long search in April 1992, the *San Antonio Express-News* found him living quietly on the south side, retired from his days as the Alamo City's favorite street performer. The drums are silent now, as is his spot at the corner of Market and Alamo Streets, but the music of Bongo Joe lives forever in the memories of the thousands who witnessed this gifted street musician.

Six Famous People Who Spent Time in San Antonio

1 Pope John Paul II

On September 13, 1987, the eyes of the world focused on San Antonio when Pope John Paul II stopped here during his second visit to the United States.

Months of planning was required to handle security, transportation, and sanitary concerns for the visit. A mass site to accommodate an expected 500,000 worshippers was chosen in the then-undeveloped area of Westover Hills.

Two obstacles prevented it from being a perfect day. First, an overly cautious public health official expressed her concerns to the local media that due to the stifling heat, hundreds would die at the papal mass site. Fortunately, her fears were unfounded, but they managed to persuade enough people to stay away that the crowd was a more manageable 350,000. And despite wearing heavy robes and a miter, the pope stayed cool thanks to a special air-conditioned chair.

Second, a few days before the event, heavy winds toppled two towers that framed the stage for the mass. There was little time to rebuild the towers, so cranes were brought in to support the remaining backdrop.

The only ones disappointed were those hoping to capitalize on the pope's visit. Despite the hundreds of thousands of visitors who flocked to the city, the worshippers chose not to buy papal lawn sprinklers (dubbed "Let Us Spray"), paper papal hats, "pope-sicles," and other cheap souvenirs that could be found on every street corner.

In spite of an early rush on accommodations and concerns that there might be a lodging shortage, most hotels ended up with a lot of empty rooms. Many pilgrims stayed with host families who volunteered their homes through local churches of every denomination.

The pope's itinerary in San Antonio included a visit to Assumption Seminary, where he had lunch with the bishops of Texas, and a visit to Plaza Guadalupe on the west side, one of the poorest sections of the city. There he spoke on the importance of parish life. The first Polish pope ended his day back at Assumption Seminary, where he met a delegation of Polish Americans from Panna Maria. Thousands also lined the streets to watch his motorcade drive to various appointments. Without a doubt, the visit of Pope John Paul II touched every person in San Antonio in some way.

2   Phil Collins

When rock star Phil Collins was growing up in London, he watched the 1950s Disney series featuring Fess Parker as Davy Crockett. This kick-started his fascination with the Alamo, which Collins refers to as "a love affair" that he's had with the Shrine of Texas Liberty since he was about five years old.

In 1973, when his band Genesis was touring the United States, Collins scheduled a day off to visit San Antonio. "I was just spellbound when I first saw it in person," he recalled. "Having lived all my life, to see it in books and movies and the pictures in magazines, it was really quite extraordinary."

His wife at the time bought him his first artifact in the 1990s. Over the years his collection grew to over 200 items valued at millions, including Davy Crockett's rifle and Jim Bowie's knife. "Some people would buy Ferraris. Some people would buy houses. I bought old bits of metal and old bits of paper," Collins said.

On June 20, 2014, Collins announced that he was donating his collection to the state of Texas for display at the Alamo. "It's at my home, in my basement in Switzerland. I look at it every day, but no one else was enjoying it." He pledged that he would continue to purchase artifacts and donate them after a period of time.

3 Charles Lindbergh

Charles A. Lindbergh flew his own private plane to San Antonio's Stinson Field on March 24, 1924, and entered the army as a cadet at Brooks Field. The number of aviators who started training on the Jenny aircraft was 104. However, in September, only 34 cadets advanced to the next step of training at Kelly Field, where they trained on the more powerful De Havilland aircraft.

Nine days before his graduation, Lindbergh had an accident and had to bail out of his aircraft. Luckily, he was a member of the first class of cadets who'd trained with a newfangled invention called the parachute (he was the twelfth military person ever to use one). On March 25, 1925, he graduated at the top of his class and accepted a second lieutenant commission and an assignment in the Air Service Reserve Corps.

A park was named for the famed aviator on Kelly Air Force Base and is now an office park site at Port San Antonio.

4 Pola Negri

Many celebrities traveling through San Antonio become enchanted with the Alamo City's charm. Occasionally, someone is so taken by the city that they decide to make it their home. Such was the case with silent film star Pola Negri.

Negri was born Barbara Apolonia Chałupiec in Lipno, Poland, where she was a star of stage and screen in Eastern Europe. She became one of the first foreign film stars to achieve success in Hollywood, appearing in such silent classics as *Bella Donna, The Spanish Dancer, Forbidden Paradise, Shadows of Paris, Woman on Trial,* and *A Woman of the World.* Her most famous role was that of Carmen in the classic *Gypsy Blood.* Her first talking motion picture was *Woman Commands.* She was often linked romantically with many of Hollywood's most famous leading men, including Charlie Chaplin. Her one great love was for Rudolph Valentino, who died in 1926.

She lived in Europe in the 1930s and returned to the United States during the Second World War. In 1957 she visited San Antonio with her friend Margaret West and was so taken by it that in 1959 she moved to the city and mostly retired from show business. Despite many motion picture offers, she preferred to lead a quiet life writing her memoirs and enjoying local life. She accepted one final offer in 1968, a Disney project titled *The Moon-Spinners.* In 1968 she was awarded the HemisFair Film Festival Award for her contributions.

Many believed that Negri was a recluse, a faded star who jealously guarded her privacy. Such was not the case. An active member of the community, she was on the board of directors of the San Antonio Symphony and of San Antonio Little Theater. She was a member of St. Anthony's Catholic Church and a supporter of the Our Lady of Czestochowa Shrine on the city's southeast side. In 1964 she donated her 700-volume library containing many rare books to Trinity University, and in 1970 she donated her rare recording collection to St. Mary's University. She contributed to Henry Cisneros's campaign for mayor in 1984 and died in San Antonio in 1987.

5 Antonio López de Santa Anna

Yes, *that* Santa Anna, from the Battle of the Alamo. After his surrender in San Jacinto, Santa Anna lived in a variety of places, including Cuba and Staten Island, New York. His time in San Antonio is well documented. What is lesser known is his role in the invention of chewing gum.

According to Jennifer Mathews's book *Chicle: The Chewing Gum of the Americas, from the Ancient Maya to*

William Wrigley, Santa Anna was trying to find a way to fund a return to the presidency of Mexico while living in New York. He had brought with him from Vera Cruz a supply of chicle—a chewy snack made out of sapodilla sap. With the assistance of amateur inventor Thomas Adams, Santa Anna tried to create a valuable substitute for rubber using chicle. When their attempt failed, Santa Anna returned to Mexico, penniless. Adams, left with a large supply of chicle, cut it into bite-size pieces and sold it as candy. Adams called his treat Chiclets and eventually made his fortune. The rest is history.

6 Rube Waddell

On Block 5, Lot 182, Space 2 of the Mission Burial Park South in San Antonio sits the rather impressive grave of George Edward "Rube" Waddell. The grave site doesn't get many visitors. Few in San Antonio remember him or know he is buried here. If not for the generosity of baseball team owner H. J. Benson and baseball legend Connie Mack, who paid for the monument, Rube Waddell would still be interred in an unmarked pauper's grave.

Who is Rube Waddell? Perhaps the greatest left-handed pitcher of all time. Waddell played in the major leagues from 1897 to 1910. He was the only pitcher to win ten games in one month (July 1902, Philadelphia Athletics) and the first to strike out three batters with nine consecutive pitches.

Other amazing statistics include
- A lifetime ERA of 2.16
- A career total of 50 shutouts
- Four 20-win seasons
- The record for strikeouts in a season (349)
- A career total of 2,316 strikeouts, 193 wins, and 261 complete games

Elected to the Baseball Hall of Fame in 1946, Waddell was arguably the first star in the fledgling endeavor known as professional baseball. Biographer Alan Howard Levy noted: "He was among the game's first real drawing cards, among its first honest-to-goodness celebrities, the first player to have teams of newspaper reporters following him, and the first to have a mass following of idol-worshiping kids yelling out his nickname like he was their buddy." Many say the upstart American League would not have survived without the draw of Rube Waddell.

It was not his blazing fastball and terrific curve that earned him fans' endearments and his nickname Rube, but rather his eccentric behavior. Often described as having the emotional and intellectual maturity of a child, Waddell was a constant source of grief for his managers. Between pitching performances, he would often disappear for days and be found playing in pickup games with neighborhood children. Once he disappeared from spring training in Jacksonville and was found leading a parade. Opposing players often distracted him on the mound with shiny objects and puppies, which were said to put him in a trancelike state. He was so bad with his money that one year the Philadelphia Athletics paid him in dollar bills to keep him from spending it too fast. He had a fascination with fires and could often be found assisting local firefighters. Many feel that he probably suffered from a social disorder.

In 1911 Waddell caught pneumonia after helping the town of Hickman, Kentucky, stave off floodwaters from an icy river. He was diagnosed with tuberculosis and, in 1913, was sent to San Antonio to live with his sister and later to a sanatorium to recover. (It's often falsely reported that he was sent to a mental institution.) In 1914 he passed away and was buried in a poorly marked grave. The faded wooden slab with his name was found by a preacher, who alerted Benson. Thanks to the efforts of Benson and numerous baseball fans, an elaborate gravestone now marks Rube Waddell's grave.

Ten Places Every San Antonian Should Know

1 Buckhorn Saloon

Few saloons are as famous as the Buckhorn. During the Wild West days, it was legendary and a unique part of San Antonio lore. It was even immortalized in Larry McMurtry's Pulitzer Prize–winning novel *Lonesome Dove.* The bar still exists today, but it has gone through many incarnations.

When Albert Friedrich opened the Buckhorn Saloon in 1881 on Dolorosa Street, the bar immediately attracted trappers, cowboys, cattlemen, and traders, who often traded horns for drinks. Soon the bar was filled with horns, and the legacy grew. Its vast horn collection included a seventy-eight-point deer rack and a host of other oddities.

In 1922 the bar moved to Houston and S. Flores Streets. During Prohibition, the Buckhorn survived by becoming more of a curio shop where everybody wanted to see the amazing collection of horns and oddities. One of the most unusual attractions was a stuffed gorilla that greeted customers as they walked in the door and often scared them, since most had never seen such a creature before.

In 1956 the Buckhorn's entire collection was bought and moved to the Lone Star Brewery. Redubbed the Buckhorn Hall of Horns, it made the transition to a full-fledged tourist attraction. The collection of horns, fins, and feathers was displayed along with a replica of the Buckhorn bar. The original back part of the bar was also relocated from the Houston Street location.

Stroh's bought the Lone Star Brewery in 1997 and moved the brewing operation to Longview. At first they kept the Hall of Horns open, but they soon decided to get out of the tourist business. The collection was sold again, this time to a group of investors led by Mary Friedrich Rogers, granddaughter of Albert Friedrich.

A new Buckhorn opened downtown in 1998 at 315 Houston Street. The working bar features an original 1913 National Cash Register machine and a 1909 cigar lighter from the original location. The gorilla that once scared customers has a new home upstairs in the African exhibit. A retro vertical outdoor sign beckons to people on the street, symbolizing that the Buckhorn Bar is back.

2   Tower Life Building

For over eighty years, the Tower Life Building has been the signature of San Antonio's skyline. Erected in 1929 on the corner of St. Mary's and Villita Streets, it was the tallest building west of the Mississippi River until the 1950s. It dominated downtown and could be seen throughout the city.

The structure was originally known as the Smith-Young Tower after its builders, the Smith Brothers and their partner, lawyer J. W. Young. The Smith Brothers purchased the land that used to be Bowen's Island in 1923 in hopes of building a complex that would equal the impact of Rockefeller Center in New York. The centerpiece was to be the Smith-Young Tower. The Bowen's Island Skyscrapers (as the project was known in its early stages) included the Plaza Hotel (now the Granada Homes), the Federal Reserve Bank (now the Mexican Consulate), the A. B. Frank Company Wholesale and Drygoods Building (now the City Public Service Building), a Chevrolet dealership, and a Montgomery Ward. Most of the buildings, including the tower, were designed by Atlee B. Ayres and his son Robert M. Ayres.

Numerous features set the tower apart from other skyscrapers. According to promotional literature, it offered the finest elevator service in the world. If you walk into the lobby today (which is virtually unchanged), you'll notice the original elevator doors, complete with the old Smith-Young logo.

This photo depicting a meteor that hit the Smith-Young Tower ran in the *San Antonio Light* on April Fool's Day 1938.

The building also featured observation decks on the seventh, twenty-second, twenty-seventh, and thirtieth floors. They have long since been closed to the public, but workers in the building still occasionally sneak out onto the thirtieth-floor deck. At one time, for fifty cents, you could ride the elevator to the twenty-eighth floor and walk up a flight of stairs to the best view in Texas. Many of the patrons who visited the observation deck have scratched their names in the copper moldings, and their etchings are still visible today.

A discerning eye will also notice some figures that circle the upper floors of the building. These are carved gargoyles that were added to protect the building from evil spirits. The practice seems antiquated now but was quite common in its day.

The Tower Life Building has had its share of historic moments. Dwight D. Eisenhower and the Third U.S. Army had its offices there in 1941. The building has also been used for everything from a mooring mast for a blimp to a performance site for a duo of aerialists.

At the time of its construction, San Antonio was experiencing an unprecedented building boom that reflected the optimism of the city in the 1920s. This explosion of new construction was halted by the Depression, and the San Antonio skyline remained virtually unchanged for the next fifty years.

Other buildings erected in this boom era include the Frost National Bank Building (1922), the Medical Arts Building (1926), the Milam Building (1928), the Express News Building (1929), the Majestic Theatre (1929), the Nix Medical Building (1929), and the Alamo National Bank Building (1929).

3   The world's first air-conditioned building

In 1928 the Milam Building was built on the corner of Travis Street and Soledad. This twenty-one-story high-rise was the first building in the world to be totally air-conditioned, accomplished in part by hauling huge chunks of ice to the basement.

So new was the idea of air-conditioning that advertisements had to be placed in local newspapers to convince businessmen of the comfort of the new system:

> At the time I moved in, I was a little prejudiced against the air conditioning system. I don't know why, for I had never taken the time to investigate it. But after moving in, I prize it above all other features in the building. Because of the air conditioning system, I can keep my windows closed and keep out the street noise. This absence of noise . . . makes this the most restful building. Then, too, with the windows closed, I can keep the wind out. If there is anything that is irritating to me it is to have my papers blown out of order. Here I can lay the lightest papers about my desk without fear. (Earl Wilson, R. E. Wilson Co., *San Antonio Evening News,* November 9, 1928)

The original air-conditioning system lasted more than sixty years.

Though downtown has changed over the past few decades, the Milam Building, with its huge Texas flag flying above it, continues to be one of the city's most prestigious addresses.

4 San Pedro Springs Park

Located across the street from San Antonio College, San Pedro Park has a special place in local history. The San Antonio Parks Department claims this often neglected piece of city property is the second oldest park in the country, behind Boston Commons.

Father Isidro Félix de Espinosa discovered the springs on April 13, 1709, during an expedition. It was he who named the springs. At the time, the water flow was so powerful that many mistook San Pedro Creek for the San Antonio River. In 1729 King Philip V of Spain declared through his viceroy in Mexico that the headwaters of the San Pedro were public land.

For years the area was a popular camping spot for travelers. The military often used it for its troops. Soldiers camped there in 1846 during the Mexican-American War, and during the Civil War, the Confederate army used the grounds as a POW camp.

The city's first zoo opened there in 1910. In 1922 the city's first swimming pool was built there on the lake bed, and a bridge that spanned the lake was incorporated into the design of the modern pool. The springwater fed the pool and flushed it out every eight hours. In 1929 the city's first branch library was established in San Pedro Springs Park. In that same year the San Antonio Little Theater opened in the northwest corner of the park, built to resemble the old Market House downtown, which had been torn down years earlier. In the 1990s the spring-fed pool was restored, replacing a 1950s-era chlorinated pool.

The park is also home to the McFarlin Tennis Center, which was once home to the San Antonio Racquets, 1986 champions of World Team Tennis. The park was listed on the National Register of Historic Places in 1979.

5 Travis Park

Travis Park is the second oldest park in the city and one of the oldest in America. It is no larger than a city block, and it is located downtown at the corner of Navarro and Travis Streets across from the St. Anthony Hotel. The land for the park was donated by Samuel Maverick, one of the only Alamo defenders to survive the infamous battle, having been sent to sign the Texas Declaration of Independence. He later established a home near the Alamo (the current site of the Gibbs Building at the corner of Houston and Alamo Streets). The land that is now Travis Park was his orchard.

In the 1950s there was a push to convert the park into a parking garage, even though the deed to the city specified that the land be used only as a park. This was followed by a proposal to build an underground parking garage and leave the park intact, but the Maverick family filed suit to protect the park. A great-granddaughter of Samuel Maverick, who was in the sixth grade at the time, organized a Save Travis Park letter-writing campaign of schoolchildren. That sixth grader, Marjo Rogers, later became the first director of the San Antonio Park Partners.

6 City Hall

San Antonio's city hall is one of the oldest in Texas. It was built between 1888 and 1891 in the middle of Military Plaza. The construction of the facility ended the open-air market and the public gatherings that were popular there for almost a century.

The original hall, designed by St. Louis architect Otto Kramer, is strikingly different from its present appearance. It was once a three-story building with a domed octagonal clock tower in the center. Two of the corners supported conical towers, while the other corners had mansard rook towers. One of the entrances had a two-story portico and a balcony for the second floor. However, when a fourth floor was added in 1927, the towers and the portico were removed, leaving the building without its most striking features. A discriminating eye can determine how the original corner towers fit onto the three-story version of the city hall.

7 Chapel of the Miracles

While driving into downtown from the north side via I-10, motorists may notice a small chapel near the San Antonio Independent School District Food Processing Plant. This small, unsanctioned, privately owned church is one of the city's oldest religious institutions, the Chapel of the Miracles, also known as the Ximenes Chapel. Once a thriving area, the land around the small church has been cleared in the name of urban renewal, and only the chapel has been spared.

Built beside San Pedro Creek in the early 1870s by a Canary Islander, the chapel has long been the destination of those seeking miracles. The crucifix, known as El Señor de los Milagros, came from Spain to be housed in Mission de Valero and is believed to have been relocated from the San Fernando Cathedral after a fire in 1813. Over the years many blind, deaf, and crippled souls have claimed they were cured by this crucifix, which is believed to be over 400 years old. The chapel is only thirty by forty feet, but its small size means little to the people who believe in its powers. It sits on Haven for Hope Way off the I-10 access road and is open most days.

8 Jefferson High School

When it was completed in 1932, Jefferson High School was years ahead of its time. Built on the edge of town (the school is now firmly surrounded by the city), the school cost the unheard-of sum of $1.5 million. The Moorish design came complete with many amenities new to the San Antonio Independent School District. It has two gymnasiums, built-in lockers, tile floors, wrought iron balconies, fountains, a 2,000-seat auditorium, and a prominent tower that overlooks the campus.

The school was such a masterpiece that *Life* magazine featured it in its March 7, 1939, issue. Gracing the cover was the Lasso Girls drill team (who later that year would perform at the New York World's Fair). The popular publication proclaimed Jefferson to be "the new elite in American high schools" and boasted about the school's three orchestras, its top-notch ROTC drill teams, and its unique courses, such as radio broadcasting (which later would produce local disc jockey Bruce Hathaway and journalist Jim Lehrer). Located on the "Texas Prairie," the school was said to have more playing fields than many Texas colleges.

Two movies were filmed there: *High School* (1937) and *Texas Girl* (1939). For years it was a tradition for students to view the films annually in the school's spacious auditorium. In 1983 the student council got the school declared a Texas Historic Landmark, and it is listed in the National Register of Historic Places.

9 La Villita

La Villita is the oldest neighborhood in the city. It was once populated by Spanish soldiers stationed at the Mission San Antonio de Valero (aka the Alamo). After a flood in 1819 the village was built with more up-to-date homes. It later became a neighborhood for German immigrants who populated the city in the latter portion of the nineteenth century. By the 1930s the area had become what could best be described as a slum. With money from the Depression-era WPA and under the leadership of Mayor Maury Maverick, La Villita was restored and revitalized. Today it is home to numerous festivals, including Fiesta's popular Night in Old San Antonio.

10 El Mercado

For many San Antonians, life without weekly trips to the H-E-B seems unimaginable. But 100 years ago, the majority of residents shopped in the marketplace. The most colorful one was the Mexican Market. Much of the market still exists as El Mercado, but it is drastically different from the bustling shops that once existed there.

The Mexican Market consisted of many parts. There was Haymarket Plaza, or the Haymarket. This majestic building stood on the corner of Commerce and San Saba Streets. The farmer's market took place here, and for quite some time the chili queens were a part of the scene. The building that dominated Haymarket Plaza is now gone, replaced by a new structure that serves as both a farmer's market and a parking lot. The Municipal Market House still stands at the corner of Santa Rosa and Commerce. In its heyday, it was the section of the market that specialized in meats and fresh-cut flowers. Today the building is a main part of El Mercado but is used primarily as a place to sell Mexican souvenirs. Produce Row, which runs through the center of El Mercado, was aptly dubbed for the abundance of fruits and vegetables sold there. Produce was also sold at Washington Square across Market Street.

Eleven Facts about the Menger Hotel

Located on Alamo Plaza, the Menger Hotel is rich with history. Originally opening the building as a brewery, William Menger soon saw the need for a first-class hotel in the Alamo City. Opening on February 2, 1859, the Menger Hotel gave San Antonio the first hotel classified as "first class" west of the Mississippi. The following are some unusual footnotes in the hotel's history.

1 The Roosevelt Bar is an exact replica of the one in the House of Lords in London. The bar was once in the front of the hotel, then was moved to a newer part of the hotel on Crockett Street. The photos on the wall of the bar depict San Antonio in its early days.

2 The Roosevelt Bar is named for Teddy Roosevelt, who recruited his Rough Riders in the hotel bar and lobby. Officially known as the First U.S. Volunteer Calvary, the Rough Riders were organized in 1898 and trained in south San Antonio in the area now occupied by Roosevelt Park and Riverside Golf Course. In 1905 President Roosevelt and his men returned to San Antonio for a reunion at the Menger.

3 The hotel guest list includes presidents Teddy Roosevelt, Taft, McKinley, Lyndon Johnson, Reagan, Truman, Eisenhower, Nixon, Bush, and Clinton; film stars John Wayne, Joan Crawford, James Stewart, Robert Mitchum, Bob Hope, José Ferrer, Sarah Bernhardt, Steve McQueen, and Linda Evans; and army generals Houston, Sherman, Pershing, Grant, and Lee.

4 The Menger has served up many unusual foods, including turtles from the San Antonio River.

5 If you have ever seen Rock Hudson, James Dean, and Elizabeth Taylor in the film *Giant,* you may have noticed the large painting in Hudson's den depicting a prairie scene. It was borrowed from the Menger and hangs on the second floor of the original building.

6 The hotel's King Ranch Suite is named after the famous King Ranch. Captain Richard King died while staying at the Menger in 1885. The room has changed little since his death, with a four-poster canopy bed dominating the room. Another suite received its name from famous guests. The Roy Rogers Suite, decorated in rawhide and leather furnishings, hosted the famous cowboy and Dale Evans during their movie-making days.

7 Mysterious tunnels occupy the ground underneath the original part of the hotel. The walls are two to three feet thick, and the tunnels once served as cold storage for the old brewery. It is rumored that one of the tunnels leads to the Alamo and was used as an escape route during the historic siege. This, of course, is unfounded because the Menger was built twenty-three years after the fall. The truth is that one of the tunnels is part of the old Alamo Madre Ditch, an ancient acequia that once served the mission.

8 Stone for the original part of the hotel was taken from the rock quarry on the north side of town, which is now the Sunken Gardens.

9 Poet Sidney Lanier wrote about San Antonio while boarding at the Menger. Writer O. Henry often mentioned the Menger in his many pieces about the city.

10 At one time, alligators were kept on the Menger's patio. The most famous was called Old Bill Menger, given to the hotel by a guest unable to pay his bill. Old Bill lived for fifty years and became quite a beloved fixture. He died in the 1930s when he got in a tussle with another patio gator.

11 In the 1940s the Menger had fallen on hard times and almost became a parking lot. It had lost much of its prestige and needed extensive repairs. Prospective buyers purchased an option on the downtown landmark in 1940 and announced that it would be razed. An outcry of support arose from across the country, and the option was dropped. The hotel was later purchased by W. L. Moody of Galveston, who restored the building.

San Antonio's Three Most Historic Hotels Not Named the Menger

The St. Anthony

Named in honor of the city's patron saint, San Antonio de Padua, the St. Anthony is both a Texas and National Historic Landmark. Built across from Travis Park in 1909 by cattlemen B. L. Naylor and A. H. Jones, the hotel was an instant success. Soon a second wing and three more stories were added. In 1936 railroad tycoon R. W. Morrison purchased the hotel with the aim of making it one of the nation's greatest. He added a third wing in 1941 and adorned it with antiques and fine works of art, including paintings by Remington, Cartier, De Young, and James Ferdinand McCann. Perhaps the most famous piece is the rosewood and bronze Steinway piano in the lobby, bought from the Russian embassy in Paris when it was selling assets to pay its war debts.

Throughout the years the St. Anthony has hosted such guests as Franklin D. Roosevelt, Ronald Reagan, Bob Hope, Princess Grace of Monaco, and John Wayne. A suite is named in honor of Wayne, a frequent guest. Samuel Gompers, founder of the American Federation of Labor, died at the hotel after returning from an international labor conference in Mexico.

The hotel was the first air-conditioned hotel in the world, the first with a drive-up registration desk, and the first to use automatic doors.

The Gunter

Another downtown hotel listed on the National Register of Historic Places, the Gunter was built in 1909 and was the city's largest building at that time. The Gunter was the city's only steel structure and featured such innovations as a central heating system, four elevators, and complete baths in 70 percent of the rooms. In 1917 a ninth floor was added, and three more stories were built in 1927. Located at the corner of St. Mary's and Houston Streets, the hotel has long been a center for visiting cattlemen. In 1921 San Antonio's most disastrous flood dumped six feet of water in the lobby.

Hilton Palacio Del Rio

When the 1968 World's Fair was awarded to San Antonio, the city was in desperate need of modern hotel rooms. It had been almost thirty years since the last hotel was built downtown. When builder H. B. Zachry stepped forward with plans for a new hotel between the River Walk and Alamo Street, he had less than nine months to do the job.

The Hilton Palacio Del Rio had to be completed in record time. Using new monolithic modular construction techniques, a tower was built in the middle of the hotel. Meanwhile, rooms were built on a site seven miles away, equipped with furniture, carpeting, lamps, TVs, and even a Gideon Bible in the nightstand. Crews worked around the clock to stack the rooms on top of each other via steel cables to lift the structures into place.

Zachry and his wife rode on the balcony of the first room as a crane lifted it into place. The builder had planned to stack ten rooms a day, but workers became so skilled at operating the special crane that by the end they were lifting thirty-five a day, enabling them to finish construction ahead of schedule. The entire project ended up taking just 202 working days—less than seven months.

Hotels That Started as Something Else

La Mansión del Rio

St. Mary's University on the city's northwest side had modest beginnings. On the banks of the San Antonio River, four Marianist brothers from the Society of Mary opened St. Mary's Institute on August 25, 1852, above a livery shop on the southwest corner of Military Plaza. It moved to its permanent home, which is now part of La Mansión del Rio Hotel, on March 1, 1853. Once the city's largest building complex, the school was originally for boys and did not become completely coed until 1963.

St. Mary's expanded to its present site in Woodlawn Hills in 1894, offering instruction in grades five through fourteen. The Woodlawn campus, known as St. Louis College, was located far outside the city. Students had to take a bus to the corner of Woodlawn and Cincinnati and walk "the longest mile in Texas" to reach the school. The downtown facility was a high school for boys known as St. Mary's Academy. In 1932 it moved to N. Main and became Central Catholic High School and St. Mary's University. St. Mary's Law School operated there from 1934 to 1966, before it relocated to the Woodlawn campus. The school has educated eight San Antonio mayors.

In 1968 the River Hotel Company turned the old school into a hotel in time to house HemisFair visitors. The building retained the style of the old college. If you walk into the courtyard, you can easily identify the old schoolhouse. La Mansión del Rio has been designated a Texas Historic Site and has received a San Antonio Conservation Society Award. The main dining room in the hotel is named Las Canarias after the Canary Islanders who founded the city.

The Emily Morgan

This neo-Gothic building on Alamo Plaza was originally a small private hospital and a variety of medical offices. Erected in 1926 and designed by Ralph Cameron, this thirteen-story building has long towered over its historic neighbor. Three generations of San Antonians have memories of the doctors who once occupied the building. The elaborate Gothic detail reflects the structure's earlier use. The faces that surround the first and second floors depict patients suffering from different ailments. In 1978 the building was renovated into office space and renamed the Landmark Building.

In 1983 the Landmark was purchased by a group of investors who intended to turn it into a hotel. Since the inside of the building had already been gutted, the only vestiges of the old Medical Arts Building were the mail chute, the brass elevators, the original floor tiles, and a staircase. It took eighteen months and $17 million to turn the former office space into the Emily Morgan, a 177-room hotel that caters more to couples than to the business traveler. Each room features a whirlpool bath.

The hotel was originally named for the famed Yellow Rose of Texas, who allegedly tipped off Sam Houston that Santa Anna was planning an attack on San Jacinto, and its name has been a source of controversy. Some say Emily Morgan was a traitor and a prostitute, others say Santa Anna was caught by surprise the morning of the attack because he was in bed with Morgan, and still others doubt her existence. Many objected to naming a penthouse suite after Santa Anna. While some find it ironic, others find it offensive that the general who defeated the defenders of the Alamo should have a suite named in his honor, especially when it overlooks the Alamo. In the early 1990s the inn was renamed the Alamo Plaza Hotel; later, new investors restored the Emily Morgan moniker.

Other hotels

The last thirty years have seen numerous empty buildings come back to life as hotels and inns. Thanks to the city's exploding tourist industry, historic property with River Walk access has become too valuable to abandon. The most dramatic restoration is the Havana Building on Navarro Street. Constructed in 1914 to house wholesale grocery buyers, it was originally known as the Edward Franz Melcher Building. In 1926 it was sold and became the Havana Rooming House. Vacant through the 1980s and most of the '90s, it was downtown's most mysterious eyesore. It took months for developers to find out who owned the property. In 1997 it reopened as the exclusive Havana Riverwalk Inn.

Across from the Aztec Theater on St. Mary's Street is the Petroleum Commerce Building, designed by Atlee B. Ayres and home of City Public Service in the 1950s. After sitting vacant for more than a decade, the Drury Inn and Suites River Walk Hotel opened in the 1990s. Similarly, a block away, the headquarters of the San Antonio Drug Company was converted to a Homewood Suites after more than ten years of vacancy. Other historic building makeovers include Alamo National Bank's transformation into the Drury Plaza Hotel and the renovation of the former City Central Bank and Trust Company building to become a Home2 Suites by Hilton. And the Bexar County Jail, built in 1878, is now a Holiday Inn Express on Camaron Street.

Old Places, New Uses

Many cities in the 1950s postwar boom tore down historic buildings in the name of urban renewal. Because of San Antonio's stagnant growth during that period, the city retained numerous structures that were later adapted for new uses.

The Pearl, formerly the Pearl Brewery

For over a century, the Pearl Brewery has been an integral fiber in the rich fabric of San Antonio. It was once the biggest brewery in Texas and one of the largest in the nation, with Pearl beer being delivered all over the country. In 1985 the brewery and the brand were taken over by Pabst Brewing Company. In 2001 Pabst became a virtual brewer, shutting down all its plants, including the Pearl. The Miller Brewery in Fort Worth was hired to produce Pearl beer, which is now sold mainly in Texas. San Antonians feared that the iconic brew house would be leveled. But in 2001 Silver Ventures purchased the property and converted it into a place where people could live, shop, and dine.

The signature building in the Pearl is the nineteenth-century brew house, which has been converted to the 146-room, four-star boutique Hotel Emma. The hotel is named after Emma Koehler, who ran the company during its glory days and kept the brewery in business during Prohibition by producing a variety of other products. Within minutes of Prohibition ending on September 15, 1933, Emma Koehler had a hundred trucks and twenty-five railcars loaded with beer for shipment.

The Pearl has done an amazing job of mixing the old and the new, adapting structures such as the Can Recycling Building and turning them into retail and office outlets. The Can Plant is a modern apartment complex with a nod to the Pearl's past.

Built in 1894, the Pearl Stable was once home to the brewery's draft horses. An elaborate and luxurious facility, this elliptical building demonstrated the company's affluence. When trucks replaced horses, the stable was used for storage. In 1950 the brewery converted the stable to a banquet facility, naming it for one-time Pearl spokesperson Judge Roy Bean and later for his one-time crush Lilly Langtry. (Remember the Jersey Lilly?) Today the stable has been renovated to its previous elegance and is available for private functions.

The Granary Cue and Brew, a restaurant on Avenue A, was once home to Ernst Mueller, a barrel maker for the Pearl Brewery. The house was sold in 2004 and renovated to become part of the Pearl complex.

Chef Steve McHugh opened the restaurant Cured in the Pearl Brewery Administration Building, which included the brewery president's office when it was built in 1904. The one-story structure is surrounded by a modern retail and office complex.

Built in 1890, the Boehler Building, at 328 E. Josephine, was home to Fritz Boehler, a brewmaster at the Pearl Brewery. It later became a boardinghouse and a beer garden for brewery workers. Then it housed the Liberty Bar for thirty years and was known for its pronounced tilt. In 2014 the Pearl purchased and renovated it, removing its famous tilt. Other buildings adapted include the Full Goods Building and the garage.

San Antonio Museum of Art, formerly the Lone Star Brewery

Arguably one of San Antonio's greatest reclamations is the former Lone Star Brewery. No other building in San Antonio has received as much national press as the Lone Star Brewery conversion. Located on 200 W. Jones on the banks of the San Antonio River, the brewery was opened in 1903 by beer king Adolphus Busch. Busch brought architects from the finest schools in Germany to design the buildings. The Lone

Cured, formerly the administrative offices for the Pearl Brewery.

Hotel Emma, formerly the Pearl's brew house.

Star Brewing Association originally produced beer under the Alamo and Erlanger labels. By 1905 it was the largest brewery in Texas, dwarfing the area's numerous small German brewers. The glory days for the building ended in 1921 with the advent of Prohibition. For a time, a soft drink named Tango was bottled there. Later it was home of the Lone Star Ice Company and, later still, a cotton mill. After Prohibition Sabinas Brewing Company bought the Lone Star label for a new brewery being built on the south side.

The building went through a variety of uses before the San Antonio Museum Association bought the complex for a mere $375,000 in 1972. At the time, the Witte Museum was exhibiting both art and natural history. The association planned to eventually move all the art exhibits to the new museum. On July 14, 1977, the brewery officially became the San Antonio Museum of Art and was christened by Mayor Lila Cockrell with a longneck bottle. It took three years to renovate the facility into a showplace. The two towers were connected by a glass walkway, and few of the building's outstanding features have been altered. From the outside, it still resembles a brewery.

Listed on the National Register of Historic Places, the museum has won numerous restoration awards.

Tobin Center for the Performing Arts, formerly Municipal Auditorium

Municipal Auditorium was one of the city's finest public buildings. Architect Atlee B. Ayres won an award for its vintage Moorish design from the American Institute of Architects. It was built in 1926 at a cost of $1.5 million and hosted such dignitaries and celebrities as Richard Nixon, Lyndon B. Johnson, Bob Hope, Will Rogers, Dean Martin and Jerry Lewis, Al Jolson, Elvis Presley, Eleanor Roosevelt, Pope John Paul II, and Jay Leno.

The Tobin Center for the Performing Arts in 2015.

Municipal Auditorium during the 1929 winter holidays.

Designed as a memorial to those who served in World War I, it was quite impressive. But as a money maker, it was a white elephant. It was never remodeled, and over the years it fell into disrepair. In 1962 Mayor McAllister called the building a "disgrace to the city" and suggested converting it into a convention center at a cost of $5 million. When the new convention center was built in Hemisfair Plaza, the auditorium fell into the role of a second-class hall, hosting wrestling matches and rock concerts.

On January 6, 1979, flames ripped through the building. The roof and the old pipe organ were destroyed. Only the outer shell and the stage—saved by the sprinkling system—remained. At first arson was suspected, but later it was discovered that a cigarette had caused the fire. The building sat in its semi-destroyed state for three years. Some wanted it renovated into a home for the symphony. Others hoped the building would become a media production center. Many remembered the squalor of the auditorium's final years and hoped it would be torn down, arguing that it was no longer needed.

After much debate, the city decided to rebuild the facility, and it reopened as a civic jewel in 1986. Almost twenty years later the county was looking for a new performing arts facility, and a bond package, along with private donations, were provided to build a world-class arts center. The newly dubbed Tobin Center for the Performing Arts opened in September 2014 and is home to ten resident groups, including the San Antonio Ballet, the opera, and the symphony. It features a 2,100-seat performance hall with the ability to fine-tune acoustics for a variety of performances. The center also includes a 250-seat studio theater and a 600-seat outdoor plaza.

When the Municipal Auditorium was built in 1926, the River Walk had not been constructed, and like many buildings of the era, it faced away from the river. The architects who designed the Tobin Center wanted to correct that and incorporated a large public park space along the river.

H-E-B headquarters, formerly the U.S. Arsenal

This massive complex on Cesar Chavez and Main was built in 1858 as an arsenal for the U.S. Army, replacing the Alamo, which the army was using for storage. Water was originally brought to the compound by one of the acequias. During the Civil War, Confederate soldiers used the armory. In 1865 it was returned to the U.S. Army and supplied Texas troops. Additional structures were built on the site in 1916 and 1933.

In 1949 the arsenal closed. The Marine Corps Reserve used some of the buildings for many years, but for the most part, they sat vacant. In 1984 the South Texas grocery chain H-E-B began using the complex as its headquarters. H-E-B did a remarkable job in its renovation, as can be witnessed by looking at the original Marine Corps Reserve building adjacent to the H-E-B property. The walkway along the river in the King William district gives an excellent view of the restored property. The headquarters were designed to blend with the surrounding homes and the adjacent River Walk.

The only structure in the complex left untouched was a concrete building in the middle of the grounds that once stored explosives. Because of the thick walls, architects decided to leave the building in its original state. Across Main Street are other structures that were part of the original arsenal, including the Commander's House, now a senior citizen recreation center.

Westside Multimodal Transit Center, formerly the Missouri Pacific Terminal

Long known as the forgotten terminal, this beautiful building received a new life in 1988. The structure, at the west end of Houston Street in the Cattlemen's Square area, was designed by Harvey L. Page—who was also the architect for the Masonic Lodge and Temple Beth-El. The dome on the terminal was covered with copper and topped with an Indian statue. Built in 1907, it was originally the terminal for the

International and Great Northern Railway (whose name is engraved around the stained glass window). It became the Missouri Pacific Terminal in the 1930s.

The terminal was closed in 1970 when the railroad discontinued the route from Texarkana to Laredo, and the building fell into disrepair. The windows were broken, the copper was stripped from the roof, and it became a haven for day laborers, drunks, and prostitutes.

In 1982 the statue was stolen from the dome, and the terminal continued to rot. Some feared the building would be lost forever if a plan was not developed to revitalize it. Suggestions included making it into a farmer's market, the main library, a science and transportation museum, a restaurant, and a city court building. The City Employee Credit Union was able to negotiate the sale (which had always been a major stumbling block) for $7 million, and the terminal became the headquarters for the credit union in the summer of 1988. The credit union spent $3.2 million restoring it. The stained glass windows were faithfully reproduced by Joe Juarez and Diane Court of Black's Art Glass Studio. The wood framing for the copper roof took three months to replace.

As for the Indian statue, it was found on Good Friday in 1982, in a field near the station. His bow had been shattered, all his feathers were shot off, his right leg was missing, and his backside had caved in. (The hollow statue was originally believed to be solid cast iron, which made many wonder how the roof could have supported it and how someone could walk off with it.) Lucille Pratte spearheaded a five-year effort to have the statue restored, and Alan Lewis of Medina Valley Forge spent four months and $4,500 restoring it. The fifteen-foot, 200-pound statue returned to its familiar perch on April 21, 1988. When the credit union outgrew the facility, they sold it to VIA Metropolitan Transit, which converted the former train station into the Westside Multimodal Transit Station.

An interesting footnote: when Amtrak took over passenger service, the train stopped at the boarded-up station, but passengers had to buy their tickets across town at the Southern Pacific Terminal.

Sunset Station, formerly the Southern Pacific Station

Located in St. Paul's Square (1174 E. Commerce), the former Southern Pacific Station is now Sunset Station, a private event center. The Mission Revival–style building was completed in 1903. The interior has been beautifully restored and boasts a stunning stained glass window on the south side featuring the seal of Texas. The stained glass window on the north side features the emblem of the Southern Pacific Lines.

Briscoe Western Art Museum, formerly the Hertzberg Circus Museum

In 1902 Andrew Carnegie donated $50,000 to the city for a new library. Land at the corner of Market and Presa Streets was donated by Caroline Kampmann. In 1921 the building was damaged by floodwaters, and a new library was built on site and completed on August 1, 1930. The outside of the newer building is framed with quotes from noted American scholars. When the library moved to Market Street in 1968, the Carnegie Library became the Hertzberg Circus Museum, named after Harry Hertzberg, a local attorney, civic leader, and state senator. Hertzberg, an avid circus fan, began collecting items in the 1920s that were donated by visiting circus performers who often dined with him and his wife as they were passing through town. After his death in 1940, his collection was donated to the public library with a stipulation that if the city could not maintain the collection, it would pass to the Witte Museum.

Due to the poor shape of the building, the museum closed in 2001, and the collection was transferred to the Witte in 2003. Shortly thereafter, a plan was developed to upgrade the former library and transform it into a museum of western art.

Lake/Flato architects produced a stunning design with dramatic gallery space facing the River Walk. Public funding and private donations, including $4 million from former Texas governor Dolph Briscoe, helped create the Briscoe Western Art Museum, which opened in 2013.

Plaza San Antonio's conference center, formerly the German-English School

The Marriott Plaza San Antonio Hotel on the corner of Cesar Chavez and S. Alamo Streets uses one of the city's oldest school buildings as its conference center. The structure, across S. Alamo from Beethoven Hall, was originally a school for the children of German intellectuals who lived in the Little Rhine section of the city. The school was built in 1859 by Johann H. Kampmann (who also built the Menger and the Lone Star Brewery). A third building was added in 1869. The school was incorporated as the German-English School of San Antonio and modeled after the German gymnasium system. The institution had two principles: no religion was to be taught, and German and English were to be equally emphasized. The curriculum was challenging and the discipline stiff. The school, facing financial difficulties and an improved public education system, closed in 1897.

The property was bought by Hilda and F. Groos, who sold it to George W. Brackenridge. In 1903 Brackenridge deeded the grounds to the San Antonio Independent School District, which opened it as Brackenridge Elementary. From 1923 to 1925 it was Page Junior High School, and in 1926 it became San Antonio College. When SAC moved to San Pedro Avenue in 1951, the building fell into disrepair. In 1968 HemisFair rescued the building from destruction and used it for office space. After HemisFair, the Four Seasons Hotel was built on the corner of Cesar Chavez and S. Alamo and used the school as a conference center. Marriott owns the hotel and continues to use the German-English School for meeting space.

Southwest School of Art, formerly Ursuline Academy

Invited by Bishop Jean Marie Odin, seven nuns traveled from Galveston to downtown San Antonio and founded the Ursuline Academy. Ten acres of land were purchased on the banks of the San Antonio River, and on November 7, 1851, the city's first school for "ladies of refinement" opened. Most of the buildings were constructed during the 1850s by architect François Giraud and contractor Jules Poinsard. The first academy building, finished in 1854, is one of the few remaining examples of *pisé de terre*, or rammed-earth construction method, in the United States. Giraud was also responsible for the chapel and the three-faced clock tower. (With no development to the north, no clock face was installed facing that direction.)

After 120 years downtown, the academy was moved to Vance Jackson Road. In 1961 Link Cowan of Oklahoma acquired the property on Augusta Street from the Catholic Church. Cowan permitted a few nuns to remain living at the old campus until 1965, when he sold the property to the San Antonio Conservation Society. The society plunged deep into debt to purchase several of the buildings, which were in an extreme state of disrepair and a haven for derelicts. On February 11, 1967, a fire destroyed the day students' building, and it was all the firefighters could do to save the remaining structures.

A five-year search for a new use for the academy ended in November 1970, when the Southwest Craft Center leased the property for a dollar a year. In 1974 a $136,000 grant from the Economic Development Agency of the Commerce Department was used for restoration, and in 1975 the organization was able to purchase the property. The center, now named the Southwest School of Art, grants a four-year bachelor of fine arts degree and is home to galleries, classes, lectures, workshops, and artists-in-residence.

Lambermont

Edward Holland Terrell served as ambassador to Belgium from 1889 to 1893, and upon returning to San Antonio in

1894, he commissioned architect Alfred Giles to build a home for his bride that resembled a European castle that he admired. Located at 950 E. Grayson across from Fort Sam Houston, the palatial home had twenty-six rooms, including a library, music room, solarium, and wine cellar, and nine fireplaces. A room on the fourth floor has windows facing north, south, east, and west for a complete view of the city. Dubbed Lambermont after one of the ambassador's business associates, the family lived there until Terrell's death in 1908. Mrs. Terrell reportedly spent the rest of her life in Paris, and the home subsequently passed through the hands of many owners. As the neighborhood decayed, the castle suffered the ultimate embarrassment when it was divided into eight apartments in the mid-1970s.

In 1986 Lambermont was restored by Katherine Poulis and Nancy Jane Haley, who opened the castle as a bed and breakfast. The mother-daughter pair became admirers of such inns after a trip west, when they stayed at one in Provo, Utah. At the time they stopped to inspect the large home for sale in their neighborhood, the building had no electricity, and they had to view the rooms with flashlights. When they learned the number of bedrooms and bathrooms, they immediately thought about making it into an inn. The bed and breakfast operates today under different ownership.

The Guenther House Restaurant, formerly the Guenther residence

The original portion of this home was built in 1860 by Carl Hilmar Guenther, founder of the Pioneer Flour Mills. The private home, which housed its last residents in 1948 and was then used for storage, has been transformed into a restaurant, museum, and gift shop. The dwelling sits on the edge of the King William district on the grounds of the Pioneer Flour Mill. It took fourteen months to refurbish the home before its grand reopening on March 22, 1988. Many of the furnishings in the restaurant, including the crystal chandelier, are family-owned pieces used in the former residence.

Old Prospect Hill Missionary Baptist Church, now apartments for the elderly

This old church is one of the city's most amazing restoration and conversion projects. The city's last remaining Beaux Art–style church, located at 1601 Buena Vista, was built in 1911 to house a large congregation. As the neighborhood demographics changed, church membership shrank. In 1965 it was disbanded, and in 1980, the church was nearly destroyed by fire. Work began soon after to rehabilitate the building into housing for the elderly. The exterior is virtually unchanged, with the exception of a red dome that replaced the fire-damaged original. The inside, though, has been remodeled, leaving few signs of its heritage.

Artes Graficas Building, the Palace Livery Stable, now law offices

The original painted sign for the Palace Livery Stable can be seen faintly on the outside of this old building constructed in 1910 on Camaron Street. It has served as everything from stables and a blacksmith shop to a fireworks factory and a publishing company. It was renovated in 1980 and is now used as law offices.

The Pavilion by Hilton, formerly the Humble Oil Pavilion and the Schultze Store

Located at the west entrance of HemisFair Park, this is one of a handful of structures that was spared the wrecking ball that decimated the neighborhood earmarked for the World's Fair. Its finely detailed cast iron work was made locally, and the building is one of the city's last Italianate-style commercial buildings. During HemisFair, this old store was used as the Humble Oil Pavilion and later became a melodrama playhouse. It is currently a meeting and banquet facility for the Hilton Palacio Del Rio.

The Schultze Store symbolizes the indecision that has characterized the redevelopment of the HemisFair site. Architect O'Neil Ford wanted to save most of the neighborhood and incorporate the buildings into the World's Fair. Planners opted for a mass urban renewal project the likes of which San Antonio had never seen before or since. Entire neighborhoods, including churches, were razed.

Other readapted structures include the old Menger Soap Factory, now an office for the Soapworks Apartments downtown; the Federal Reserve Bank, which today houses the Mexican Consulate; and the Mexican American Unity Council, which occupies a seventy-year-old elementary school building in Prospect Hill. The Koehler House, once the home of Pearl Brewery heirs, is now used by San Antonio College. The Junior League has its offices in the former home of Claudius King, and the Conservation Society uses the former Anton Wulff home as its headquarters. The American Security Life building (at St. Mary's and Pecan Streets) and the Maverick, Brady, and Majestic buildings (on Houston Street) have been converted into apartment complexes. The downtown Cadillac dealership near the Central Library is now the Cadillac Lofts. One of the most unusual reuse projects is in northeast San Antonio, where Windsor Park Mall became the corporate headquarters for Rackspace.

Eight Things You Should Know about Brackenridge Park

1 **Much of the old park is a former quarry.**
That is, a former cement plant and a former Confederate tannery. Unlike most parks, Brackenridge was not pristine land

put aside for public use. Long before anyone named George Brackenridge existed, the area was used to dam the headwaters of the San Antonio River and divert it to the missions via the Acequia Madre. The zoo and the Sunken Gardens occupy the old Alamo Roman and Portland Cement quarry, which closed in 1908. The smokestack and the kiln from the old cement factory are a popular stopping point for garden visitors.

2 The park used to host a beach in the San Antonio River.

In 1915 Park Commissioner Ray Lambert designed a swimming beach in the park near the headwaters of the San Antonio River. At first the extremely popular swimming hole had a gravel bottom, but in 1924 he lined its floor with concrete and had changing rooms built for the public. He also moved the old downtown St. Mary's Street Bridge into the park near the swimming area, where it remains. Though swimming is no longer allowed, Lambert Beach still exists. The changing rooms have been converted to an imaginative playground for children, and the swimming area is mainly occupied by ducks.

3 The park is home to some priceless artworks by Dionicio Rodríguez.

Dionicio Rodríguez was arguably the master of the art form that makes concrete look like petrified wood. His pieces are scattered around San Antonio, including two in the park. On the park's north side just off Hildebrand Avenue is a "log" bridge that is still in use sixty-plus years after its construction. The second piece is the Sunken Gardens entrance gate, which forever marks San Antonio's World War II anti-Japanese hysteria.

4 The Japanese Tea Garden changed its name during World War II.

The Japanese Tea Garden, also known as the Sunken Gardens, was built in 1918 in an abandoned quarry. In 1924 Kimi Elizo Jingu, a local artist, was asked to open a restaurant

Built in 1889, this tall stack kiln was used by the Alamo Cement Company, originally located at the quarry that would become the Japanese Sunken Gardens.

there. The Bamboo Room served light lunches until 1942, when his family was evicted from the park due to anti-Japanese sentiments. The park was renamed the Chinese Tea Garden, and Dionicio Rodríguez was commissioned to build a gate with the new name. Although that gate is still on the grounds, the park was renamed the Japanese Tea Garden in 1984, and Jingu's children were invited to the rededication. After years of neglect, a major renovation starting in 2007 brought the gardens back to their original splendor.

5 Brackenridge Golf Course used to be much larger.

Construction for Brackenridge Golf Course, the city's first public course, began in 1915. It was originally large enough to host PGA events, but in the 1960s a freeway cut through the park, making the course considerably smaller. Portions of the park, including the twelfth green, were on the other side of Highway 281. The San Antonio Flood Control inlet is on a piece of land south of the highway that also used to be part of the course.

6 The San Antonio Zoo was one of the first cageless zoos.

In 1929 the zoo opened two of the country's first cageless zoo exhibits, the Barless Bear Terraces and the Primate Paradise, commonly known as Monkey Island. Built in an old quarry, this unique site houses one of the world's most innovative zoos.

7 Brackenridge Park is actually two parks.

Most know that land for the park was donated by George Brackenridge. His home was at the headwaters of the river and is still on the University of the Incarnate Word campus. Part of the parkland was also used to pump river water into the city's early municipal water system, which was owned by Brackenridge. Those two pump houses still exist.

But much of the park land was donated by Emma Koehler, the widow of the Pearl Brewery owner Otto Koehler. The north section is actually Koehler Park, named in his honor. Brackenridge stipulated that his park be dry, while Emma Koehler insisted that her adjacent park be open to serving Pearl beer and other "adult beverages."

8 The park is home to the oldest music club for women in Texas.

Founded in 1901 by Anna Hertzberg, the Tuesday Musical Club is dedicated to the discussion and performance of classical music.

San Antonio jeweler Eli Hertzberg was on a visit to New York City in 1882 when he met Anna Goodman, a classical pianist trained at the New York Conservatory of Music. Within a few weeks of their introduction, they wed and came back to San Antonio. Missing her cultural connections, Mrs. Hertzberg started an all-woman chamber music society, the first women's music association in Texas. Since 1923 the club has hosted the Artist Series, one of the nation's oldest continuous performance series hosted by women. In 1949 the Tuesday Musical Club built a new home next to the Sunken Garden Theater in Brackenridge Park.

Six Incredible Movie Palaces

Downtown was once a vibrant place for moviegoers. If you stood on the corner of Houston and St. Mary's Streets, you could see the State, the Alameda, the Texas, the Majestic, the Empire, and the Aztec. San Antonio is one of the few cities in Texas to have so many downtown theaters left.

1 Majestic Theatre

The Majestic opened in June 1929 as one of the premier palaces of its time. One Texas theater owner claimed the San Antonio

Majestic "will be as great an influence for good as the church." It was designed by Chicago architect John Adolph Emil Eberson, who created elaborate theaters across America, including four in Texas. Eberson is known as the father of the "atmospheric theater." The Majestic is recognized as his most elaborate creation.

Eberson wrote, "To be a successful theatre architect, one must be a showman. I want to create theatres where pictures can be enjoyed in restful and beautiful surroundings rather than one that would be a mere flaunt of lavishness." The theater and fourteen stories of office space were built for $2 million and took thirteen months to complete. Its switchboard was powerful enough to supply the electricity for a town of 15,000. The Majestic was initially built to host both movies and vaudeville. It closed for a short time in 1930 and reopened as a first-run movie house.

The theater's interior is a mixture of Spanish and Moorish design and includes Eberson's trademark ceiling, sky blue with twinkling stars and a parade of passing clouds produced by a concealed machine called a brenograph. The left side of the auditorium is patterned after a Spanish colonial palace, and the right side after a Moorish castle. Each side is decorated with tiled towers, plazas, false balconies, a dozen doves, and one peacock. Eberson designed the complex interior to be built with plaster. The metal- and wood-looking fixtures are all actually plaster, which was the building material of choice because it was the least expensive. The lobby comes complete with a series of balconies, staircases, a fountain with an unclothed beauty named "Sweet Grapes" by Harriet Frishmuth, and a large aquarium. One of the interesting features of the theater is the segregation-era balcony for people of color. It was only accessible from an entrance on the back street and is barely visible from the rest of the theater. The old entrance for the third balcony is still visible on College Street.

The Majestic closed in 1974 and was later transformed into a performing arts theater featuring touring rock bands and Broadway shows. In 1988 the city acquired the Majestic

The Majestic Theatre during the premier of Audie Murphy's *To Hell and Back*.

Earl Abel at the Texas Theatre organ.

and the adjacent Empire and leased them for a dollar a year to the nonprofit group Las Casas, which raised almost $5 million to restore the theater. San Antonio architect Milton Babbitt, along with movie palace restorers Ray Shephardson and Sonya White, refurbished the theater to its former elegance. Local craftsmen, some of whose fathers and grandfathers worked on the theater, were hired for the restoration. Samples of the old carpet and seat covers were found and re-loomed. Extensive work was done in the basement to provide additional dressing rooms and storage space. Space was leased in the adjacent garage to build a new bar so the lobby could be restored to its original size. The upper floors were converted into apartments. The Majestic is now home to Broadway plays and concerts.

2 Charlene McCombs Empire Theatre

The Empire, around the corner from the Majestic, was built in 1913 by Thomas Brady and is part of the Brady Building, which sits at the intersection of Houston and St. Mary's Streets. It was built for both movies and vaudeville on the site of the old Turner Opera House. Though much smaller than the Majestic, the Empire was the largest theater in town at the time. Its first film was the silent feature *Neptune's Daughter.*

The stage was originally surrounded by gold leaf, but during renovation in the 1940s the gold leaf was plastered over after a devastating flood, giving the theater a plain appearance. The Empire closed in 1978 after becoming a home to adult films. In 1988 the city purchased it and in turn leased it to Las Casas Foundation. The Empire and the Majestic were redesigned to share many support facilities, such as dressing rooms, offices, and a music library. Work on the theater itself did not begin until after the Majestic renovation was complete. Many saw the small theater as the Majestic's poor stepchild.

Because color photography was not financially viable when the Empire was built, no visual record of the theater's former beauty existed. Workers got their first surprise when they stripped off paint and plaster to reveal the gold leaf that had been hidden for fifty years. Due to lack of funds, restoration progressed slowly. In 1992 the old bronze eagle that had sat atop the marquee was found tucked away in a ladies room. The bird returned to its original perch, the mahogany railings were restored, and six and a half pounds of gold leaf restored the stage's splendor.

In 1998 the Empire reopened thanks to a $1 million donation from Charlene and Red McCombs and was renamed the Charlene McCombs Empire. The restored Empire is now home to a variety of concerts and banquets.

One person who really appreciated the renovation was Chris Crabtree, who was an usher at the Empire when he lost his wallet in 1951. Forty-one years later workers found it stashed inside a wall. His wallet was returned complete with a used ticket to the Majestic.

3 Aztec Theatre

This large theater at the corner of Commerce and St. Mary's Streets was built in 1926 as a lavish atmosphere theater. The builders sent a team of designers to Mexico to study the ancient Mayan, Aztec, and Toltec ruins. The team's drawings were used to design replicas for the interior of the theater. The Hall of Columns at Mitla was the inspiration for the foyer. Each column is topped by a mask with glowing eyes, representing the Aztec moon goddess. The lobby featured an Aztec sacrificial stone and was painted with bloodstains in the grooves to give it that authentic touch. A two-story, two-ton chandelier hung in the lobby. The original fire curtain depicted the meeting of Cortez and Montezuma. The arch separating the curtain and the orchestra pit is decorated with the symbol of Quetzalcoatl, chief god of the Aztecs. The Mayan theme is quite impressive, but it lost some of the impact when it was divided into a three-screen theater in 1964. The Aztec was the last of the old downtown palaces to show first-run movies.

Developer Hap Veltman wanted to make the theater into a performing arts center (possibly a home for the symphony) and use the Karotkin Building for condos. Veltman's death in the summer of 1988 and the redevelopment of the Majestic and the Empire put the project in jeopardy. That August the San Antonio Conservation Society purchased it, and it was finally renovated in 2007. It was used as a venue for plays and other events until 2014, when it reopened as a concert venue and a lounge.

4 Texas Theatre

The Texas Theatre, designed by the Boller Brothers, opened on December 18, 1926. (Remember, the first talking picture did not arrive until 1927.) One of the most important events in the history of the palace was the premiere of the film *Wings,* which was the first movie to win an Academy Award. The Texas was decorated in a Wild West–rococo style and featured a plaster canopy that assisted the acoustics. The canopy, a Boller Brothers trademark, was connected to the walls of a Spanish patio. At the center of the patio was a lone star, which did not stand for Texas but was the symbol of the Publix Theatre chain.

The Texas featured three balconies, the top being segregated seating. A third box office and a special concession stand were provided for black patrons. The theater also had a pipe organ, but it was removed sometime around World War II. Its walls were adorned by murals featuring the work of artist José Arpa. The Texas seated over 2,700 and hosted a variety of entertainers from Bing Crosby and W. C. Fields to a number of rock bands. It was one of only two Boller Brothers fantasy-type theaters left in existence, and many felt the auditorium was worth fighting for. Unfortunately, some Dallas developers felt differently. Republic Bank wanted to tear it down to build a block-long office plaza. Conservationists wanted the theater to be incorporated into the design and offered their own plans.

The bank said a huge auditorium did not fit into its vision but offered a compromise by hiring the firm Ford, Powell, and Associates to incorporate the old facade into the new building. The San Antonio Conservation Society offered $12 million to purchase the theater; when the offer was refused, it hired preservationist Michael Graves, who designed a skyscraper that not only saved the theater but also incorporated some of its distinctive features. Once again, the society's offer was rejected. After a series of court battles and protests, the Texas Theatre was torn down. The facade was saved, but many felt the final solution was a poor compromise that served neither party's interests. The loss of the movie house is felt more intensely now that the other downtown theaters have been renovated.

5 Alameda Theater

The Alameda Theater and International Building, built in 1949, was one of the country's last grand downtown movie palaces. Designed by architect Straus Nayfach, it was a monument to Pan-American unity and is known for its murals depicting the history of Texas and Mexico. It also has some interesting tile work inside and out. Located at 318 Houston Street, five blocks from the Majestic, the Alameda is undergoing a $22 million restoration to become a Latino performing arts center.

6 Cameo Theatre

Situated in the St. Paul Square Historic District, this theater once mainly catered to a black audience. Since the square has been restored, the theater has been used as a concert hall, small performance hall, and nightclub. It is currently a playhouse.

When downtown was the only place for entertainment in San Antonio, it featured numerous theaters. Many started out by featuring live shows and were later converted to movie palaces. Alamo Plaza features two movie houses: The Palace, at 325 Alamo Plaza, was the first theater built by the Santikos family. It closed in 1954. The Plaza Theater, next to Joske's on the corner of Blum and Alamo Plaza in the Conroy Building, closed in 1939 when the building was bought by the department store in their quest to become the biggest store in the biggest state.

The State, located at 209 Main Avenue, closed in 1959. Houston Street was by far the most popular destination for moviegoers and featured the Prince, the Rivoli, the Rialto, the Pearl, the Orpheum, the Royal, the Princess, the Jewel, and the Star. Most of these closed during the early days of the Depression.

Seven Suburban Theaters Readapted

The large complexes with more than twenty screens near Loop 1604 are actually the second wave of suburban theaters. If you look hard enough, you can find the remnants of the first wave. Though not as stunning as downtown palaces like the Majestic, these neighborhood movie houses had more atmosphere than most of the newer suburban cineplexes. None of these show first-run movies anymore.

1 The Woodlawn

Like the Majestic, this suburban showplace was designed by John Eberson's company. The Woodlawn on Fredericksburg Road in the Deco district has a place in history because it was the site for the premiere of *The Alamo* with John Wayne. It later became a second-run house, an arts house, a concert hall, and a church. Currently it is used as a community theater playhouse.

2 Teatro Guadalupe

Teatro Guadalupe, originally known as El Progreso, was built in 1942 to host movies and vaudeville performances. Located at the corner of Guadalupe and Brazos Streets, the theater was restored in 1984 to host a variety of community events. The theater and adjacent Plaza Guadalupe are at the heart of Guadalupe Cultural Arts Center.

3 The Broadway

The Broadway in Alamo Heights (4940 Broadway) stopped showing movies in the early '80s and later became a bank. Today the building houses a variety of businesses.

4 The Olmos

The Olmos, located on 4205 San Pedro, tried valiantly to survive, first as a second-run theater and then as an arts movie house. Later it showed adult films. Now home to a charter school, there is little to suggest it was once a theater.

5 The Uptown

The Uptown was sold to St. Anne's Catholic Church and is now a gym for the school. The front of the theater on Fredericksburg Road is no longer recognizable, but if you step inside, the old building reveals its former self. The gym floor is surrounded by the stage and theater trim. The lobby is now used for storage.

6 The Josephine

The Josephine, at the corner of Josephine and St. Mary's Streets, ended its career as an adult movie house. The theater sat vacant for several years and in 1988 was reclaimed as a community theater.

7 Mission Drive-in

Mission Drive-in on Roosevelt Avenue was the city's last open-air theater, and when the land was redeveloped, the iconic screen was kept. San Antonio once had several such establishments, many at the edge of town. Most have been replaced by shopping centers and apartments.

Five Places in San Antonio That Are Replicas

1 Roosevelt Bar

This bar in the Menger Hotel on Alamo Plaza is a replica of the Peers' Bar in the House of Lords in London, but this one is open to the public. The Menger owners sent an architect to London to copy the bar. It was built in 1881 at a cost of $60,000. Originally named the Menger Bar, it was later redubbed the Roosevelt Bar after Teddy Roosevelt recruited his Rough Riders there.

2 Lourdes Grotto Sanctuary

This sanctuary, an exact replica of the Shrine of Lourdes in southern France, is located on the grounds of the Oblate School of Theology at 285 Oblate Drive.

3 San Pedro Playhouse

Located in San Pedro Park and home to San Antonio's Little Theater, the front of this building is a replica of the old Market House located on Market Street in the 1850s.

4 Shrine of the Little Flower

This west side church, on the corner of Zarzamora and Kentucky, was built in 1931. A replica of a church in France, the parish is a memorial to Sister Thérèse, a cloistered Carmelite nun who was known as the Little Flower. Contributions came from around the world to cover construction costs, which were over $500,000. The altar statues are from Spain, and the Stations of the Cross were cast in Germany. The altar is made of Carrara marble. The names of those who donated money for the shrine are engraved in marble inside the church.

5 The White House

On the north side of San Antonio, just inside the loop, is a private residence that is a replica of the White House. Because it is a private residence, the author has chosen not to pass along the address—you will have to find it yourself.

Nine Structures That Have Been Moved from Their Original Sites

1 Fairmount Hotel

Originally at the location of the Marriott Rivercenter, this building was moved to make way for the new downtown shopping center. The hotel is the largest building ever moved on pneumatic tires through municipal streets. It took weeks of preparation to ready the building for the move. Emmert International of Portland, Oregon, was hired to transport the structure. Thirty-six dollies, each with eight wheels, supported thirty steel beams, which in turn supported the hotel. The entire building was wrapped in steel cables.

The mobile hotel weighed in at 1,600 tons. There was great concern that the structure would cause damage to the Market Street Bridge over the River Walk. The river had to be drained at that location, and extra supports were added to the bridge. On March 30, 1985, the Fairmount was ready to roll. The building was blessed by Auxiliary Bishop Bernard Popp before it left its resting place at Bowie and Commerce Streets. It took six days before the building reached its new home at the corner of S. Alamo and Nueva Streets.

Thousands gathered to watch the hotel make its historic journey. True to the city's reputation, San Antonians made the event something of a party for onlookers. Vendors sold food, drinks, and souvenirs to the masses. The building moved at a snail's pace. It took four hours to turn a corner, and on the straightaways, it would reach a top speed of four miles an hour. The engineers found their first success when the building passed safely over the Market Street Bridge. There were rumors circulating that Las Vegas had placed 7–1 odds against success, but gambling authorities dismissed this, saying the event was too weird to bet on. As the hotel passed the Samuel Gompers statue on Market Street, many in the crowd rooted for the structure to knock over the disliked monument. On April 4, 1985, the Fairmount reached its destination. The seventy-nine-year-old hotel, which had been abandoned for the last few years, had been saved. The building was set on a new foundation and refurbished into a first-class hotel.

2 Original Alamo National Bank Building

This building on Commerce and Soledad Streets was moved sixteen feet, in 1910, to accommodate the widening of Commerce. The widening was privately financed, and the building was moved without interrupting banking services.

3 Playland Park Chapel

Also known as the Pleasant Valley Church, this small structure located near the Playland Park roller coaster was moved, in February 1987, to its new location at Anacacho and St. Gertrudis Streets near O'Conner Road, where it has been renovated to become St. Edward's Anglican Catholic Church. The parish wanted to renovate the old chapel because it reminded them of an old English country chapel.

The chapel was built in 1964 atop one of the last sections of the Acequia Madre. It had been hidden in a corner of the park near the roller coaster and was dedicated to "everyone seeking a moment of peaceful meditation in this mixed-up world." Every half hour a recording of the Sermon on the Mount, recited by Melvin T. Munn, would play. The chapel sat vacant and deteriorated for seven years after Playland Park closed in 1980. The new congregation added stained glass windows, a new steeple, and a new altar when the building reached its new destination.

4 Playland Park roller coaster

The Playland Rocket opened in 1941 and was once the largest roller coaster in South Texas. But when Playland Park closed in 1980, the screams of delighted riders were silenced. In January 1985 Knoebel's Grove Amusement Park, in Elysburg, Pennsylvania, purchased the ride and moved it to its new location. Over $750,000 was spent to move and restore the Rocket, which was cheaper than purchasing a new roller coaster. It took almost three months to disassemble and number each piece of wood before shipping it all to Pennsylvania. The Rocket, which once was ranked as one of the ten best roller coasters, was reborn in summer 1985 as the Phoenix. Currently, the born-again ride is ranked second among *Amusement Today*'s top wooden coasters.

5 O. Henry House

The former home of William Sydney Porter, or O. Henry as he was better known, was originally located at 904 S. Presa. In 1959 its owner sold the adobe house to the San Antonio Conservation Society for one dollar, with the stipulation that the house be saved and moved to a new location. Many sites were investigated, and finally the Lone Star Brewery was chosen. The house was sold to Lone Star for one dollar in 1960 and was part of their museum for over thirty years.

When the Lone Star Brewery closed in 1997, the house passed through various hands until it was purchased and moved to the corner of Dolorosa and Laredo in downtown. The house is currently operating as a museum and is open to the public.

6   August C. Stuemke Barn

This structure, originally located at 215 N. Flores, was constructed in 1867 by August Stuemke. The two-story building was given to the San Antonio Conservation Society by Frost National Bank, along with the funds to relocate it, in 1982. Master stonemason Curtis Smith dismantled the barn and meticulously numbered and photographed every stone for reconstruction at its new location, 107 King William Street. The building is now used as a meeting place for the society.

7   Daniel Sullivan Stable and Coach House

This structure, designed by Alfred Giles and built in 1896, once stood behind one of the stately mansions that used to grace Broadway. For many years it sat in the parking lot of the *San Antonio Light* on Broadway and Fourth, but in 1988, the coach house was moved to the Botanical Gardens. After seven years it was completely restored as an entrance to the gardens.

8   John Twohig House

Banker and merchant John Twohig was called the Breadline Banker of St. Mary's for his practice of handing out bread every Saturday night to the city's poor. But he was best known for blowing up his own store on Main Plaza in 1842 to keep his stock of gunpowder from falling into the hands of Mexican invaders. Twohig's house was moved, brick by brick, from its location on St. Mary's Street downtown to a new home at the Witte Museum, in 1941. The Twohigs' house was the last WPA project completed in Texas.

9   Francisco Ruiz House

The Witte Museum also has the Francisco Ruiz house, moved from the south side of Military Plaza in 1942. Believed to have been built in 1765, it was once the home of a signer of the Declaration of Texas Independence.

Seven San Antonio Landmarks Built in Old Rock Quarries

San Antonio has a rich history of limestone production. For many cities, the number of abandoned quarries would be a quandary. For San Antonio, it was a chance to make an architectural gem.

1 **Sunken Gardens and Sunken Garden Theater**
From 1880 to 1907 this area was the site of the Alamo Portland Cement Company. Operated by Englishman William Loyd, it was the first Portland cement plant west of the Mississippi. Cement from the quarry was used in building the state capitol. When the plant was moved to Alamo Heights in 1907, the abandoned quarry was donated to the city. It sat unused for ten years, but thanks to a dream by park commissioner Ray Lambert, the scarred cavity came alive with flowers, a pagoda, walkways, and a lagoon. The old smokestack and kilns of the Portland Cement Company were incorporated into the design of the garden. Prisoners from the city jail provided the labor of building the gardens to keep the cost down. The name Japanese Sunken Gardens was given to the new facility. A Japanese couple maintained a tearoom there, but during World War II, with rising resentment toward the Japanese, the gardens were renamed the Chinese Sunken Gardens. One of the old entrances to the park still bears this name. Later the name was shortened to Sunken Gardens, until 1984, when the original name was restored.

2 **Trinity University**
Founded in 1869, Trinity University moved to San Antonio in 1942, from Waxahachie, Texas, and originally occupied the grounds of the University of San Antonio, a small Methodist institution, on the city's near west side. After ten years, Trinity moved to the present site off Highway 281 and Hildebrand

Road. The once abandoned quarry has been transformed into one of the nation's most attractive campuses, thanks to the work of architects Bartlett Cocke and O'Neil Ford.

3 Alamo Stadium

Alamo Stadium was one of the city's greatest bargains. It was built in 1940 with $370,000 from the Depression-era WPA and with an additional $100,000 from the San Antonio Independent School District. The original plan included a baseball field at one end of the grandstands, making the stadium a multipurpose L-shaped facility. The field was dedicated on September 20, 1940, in an area of town that was without much development. The governor was on hand for the festivities, and the first event was a doubleheader football game. In game one, Corpus Christi High beat Jefferson 14–0. In the second contest, Brackenridge outdueled Houston Reagan 19–2. The stadium was an instant success. Its bowl shape, lighted field, and spacious press box made it an extremely modern facility. It made enough money in eight years to pay off the bonds used for its construction. In 1950 Alamo Gym was built with the profits from the stadium. (Alamo Gym, known for many years as a sweatbox, was not air-conditioned until 1989.)

Alamo Stadium was one of many names under consideration for the facility. A citywide poll conducted by a local paper showed that "The Chili Bowl" was most popular with students. Other suggestions included Bexar Bowl, Blue Bonnet Field, Cactus Field, Huisache Bowl (named after the street), Laurel Field (after the neighborhood), Mission Stadium, San Antonio Stadium, and Hollers Field (in honor of the school board president). It's often referred to by locals as the Rockpile.

4 San Antonio Zoo

Located in Brackenridge Park, the San Antonio Zoo is one of the best zoos in Texas. An acequia provides the park's water, and the old quarries that produced stones for Spaniards' homes have been recrafted into numerous barless cages, which were some of the first in the United States when the zoo opened in 1929. The zoo has one of the world's largest collections of antelopes and cranes (including the whooping crane, of which there are fewer than 400 in the world). Many exotic animals were first bred in the United States at the San Antonio Zoo, including the American flamingo, the white rhinoceros, and the dama gazelle.

One of the zoo's innovative fund-raising efforts sprang from an unusual source—practical jokes. On April Fool's Day, the zoo's switchboard was always unusually busy with calls for Mr. C. Lyon or Mrs. G. Raffe. In the mid-1980s the Zoological Society decided to make the best of it. Now, when people call and ask to speak to Mr. L. E. Phant, phone volunteers inform the callers that they have been victims of an April Fool's gag and then ask them to make a donation to the zoo. The program has become so successful that other zoos across the country have started similar programs.

5 Six Flags Fiesta Texas and La Cantera

This amusement park, famous for the frightening Rattler roller coaster, was built in an abandoned rock quarry (*la cantera* is Spanish for quarry) at Loop 1604 and I-10. The Rattler even makes use of the old quarry wall by tunneling through the rock on its final curve. In 2013 the original wooden Rattler was replaced by the Iron Rattler. The majority of La Cantera's development, which includes a resort, an outdoor shopping mall, and two golf courses, is built in the quarry.

6 Lincoln Heights and the Quarry Market

The Alamo Portland Cement Company moved to Alamo Heights in 1907 when it outgrew its old site. When this plant was built, it was still three miles from the end of the streetcar line on a wild piece of land, so the company built its own town on the site to support it. Cementville, as it was called, had a school, a church, a company store, a YMCA swimming pool, and small frame houses. When the company moved its operation to Loop 1604 and Green Mountain Road in 1985, the company town died, and the site was sold to developers. The Cementville headquarters and lab have been redeveloped into restaurants, and the Quarry Market is in the old plant. The smokestacks were incorporated into the design of one of the retail outlets. The abandoned pit became the Quarry Golf Club.

7 Heroes Stadium, Toyota Field, and Morgan's Wonderland

The stadium for the North East Independent School District became the second one in San Antonio to be built in an abandoned quarry. NEISD bought the old Longhorn Quarry off Wurzbach Parkway in 2007 with the idea of creating a new sports complex for the district. Heroes Stadium currently has football, track, and soccer, and has plans to include a baseball stadium as well.

At one time the quarry was discussed as a site for AT&T Center and a possible new home for the Spurs and the Rodeo, but it ended up becoming Toyota Field, a soccer-specific stadium for the San Antonio Scorpions FC (Football Club) and the STAR Soccer Complex.

Both the Scorpions and the STAR Complex use their net profits to support Morgan's Wonderland, an amusement park for people with special needs; in fact, the Scorpions were specifically formed to benefit the special-needs community, the first professional sport franchise in the world with that mission. The twenty-five-acre Morgan's Wonderland opened in the former quarry in 2010 by Gordon Hartman, who wanted a place for kids of all ages to have fun, regardless of their abilities. Those with special needs and their caretakers are able to enjoy the park absolutely free.

Twelve Pieces of San Antonio That Are Gone but Not Forgotten

1   Hot Wells Hotel

As the city of San Antonio moves into its fourth century, it is without dispute that tourism has become a major part of the local economy. But a glance back into the city's history shows what San Antonio was before it became a tourist destination for the well-heeled traveler. Supplied with hot mineral water from the Edwards Aquifer, the San Antonio area sprouted many resorts in the early part of the twentieth century, not unlike those of Mineral Wells, Texas; Hot Springs, Arkansas; or Saratoga Springs, New York.

The industry began in 1892, when an artesian well containing sulfurized water was discovered at the Southwestern Lunatic Asylum (now known as the San Antonio State Hospital). The water was unfit to drink, but the board of directors realized the significance of their find and leased the water rights to a variety of operators over the years. In the late 1800s and early 1900s, mineral baths such as these became destinations for society's elite because they were thought to offer a certain therapeutic effect that provided cures for all sorts of ailments.

In 1900 a new era began for the springs as the Texas Hot Sulphur Water Sanitarium Company opened for business with Otto Koehler as president. The new company purchased the land, and by September, three new swimming pools were built—one for each gender and one for families. Additional land was bought in 1901, and a hotel was completed that year. The hotel was a three-story brick building with three wings that opened up into a courtyard. It contained eighty first-class rooms that provided modern conveniences, such as hot and cold water, steam heat, telephones to the office, electric and gas lights, and fine furnishings. Masseurs and private baths were available, as were solid porcelain tubs in addition to steam, Turkish, Russian, and Roman baths. The swimming pools were lined with white enamel bricks (a smart move considering San Antonio's lime problem). Advertisements for the spa were placed in newspapers as far away as New York and Chicago, comparing it to the best in the world.

Other attractions soon followed. An ostrich farm relocated from San Pedro Springs Park about that time. Ladies from the city and those staying at the resort would travel to the farm for feathers, which were quite the fashion statement of the period. A bowling club, featuring both nine-pin and ten-pin lanes, opened up in 1902, and in 1906 the Cincinnati Reds held spring training there. The International Fair and Exhibition at nearby Riverside Park also attracted guests until the fair closed in 1904.

The resort continued to grow. In 1906 it was reported that approximately 2,000 guests had to be turned away. Late the next year, work began on an addition that would add ninety rooms, making it one of the largest hotels in the Southwest. A new streetcar line brought visitors from downtown for a mere nickel.

Transportation propelled the Hot Sulphur Wells Resort to a new level when railroad tycoon E. H. Harriman visited in February 1909. Harriman had a spur built that connected the hotel to the main tracks of his San Antonio & Aransas Pass Railroad. In fact, he was able to take his private rail car right to the resort grounds, which he visited to improve his poor health. Although he attributed his improved health to the "crazy waters," Harriman died in September 1909. Oddly enough, a promotional book for the facility includes a letter of endorsement from Harriman dated March 1, 1910.

With the addition of the rail spur, the resort enjoyed even more success. The Star Film Company established field offices at the resort in 1911. That company, along with other filmmakers, used the area around the hotel for filming many westerns. Sarah Bernhardt arrived at the hotel in her private rail car for an extended stay with the company. Other visitors included Rudolph Valentino, Douglas Fairbanks, Will Rogers, Hoot Gibson, Tom Mix, Teddy Roosevelt, Mrs. J. P. Morgan, Cecil B. DeMille, and Porfirio Díaz, many of whom traveled via their private rail cars.

The hotel flourished until 1917. But World War I and Prohibition both had profound effects on the resort. When the elite clientele stopped coming, the management tried to lure locals in with formal dinners and orchestra performances, but the hotel faltered. During the war, it was used to house officers and their families from Brooks Field.

On January 17, 1925, the hotel building caught fire, leaving only the outer bricks intact. The fire department pumped water from the river and was able to save the bathhouse.

In 1927 the old resort was converted into the Hot Wells Tourist Court, where guests stayed in newly built cabins and were allowed to use the pool in the bathhouse. In 1942, the property became a trailer park and motel, and the old bathhouse became the Flame Room, a neighborhood bar and grill. The owners allowed swimmers in the bathhouse for one dollar. By the mid-1970s, most of the cabins were vacant and only a few permanent residents lived in the trailer park.

The Flame Room closed in 1977, and the owners agreed to sell the property to anybody willing to refurbish the hotel. On the night of June 27, 1988, flames ravaged the old bathhouse. The caretaker stated that lightning struck the steeple about 6:30 p.m. Old wooden beams and extremely dry wood fed the vicious flames for two hours.

Since the bathhouse had been condemned, there was no insurance money. Although the building was on the National Register of Historic Places, the loss to the city could not be put in terms of a dollar value. For many years afterward, the sulfur pools remained intact among the ruins. In 2014 the wells that supplied the healing waters to the pool were permanently capped. The current owners are hoping to open a spa on the site and have a portion of the grounds donated to the city for a public park.

2 The mysterious Robert Johnson

The Gunter Hotel made its place in history in 1936 when legendary blues guitarist Robert Johnson recorded there. Johnson, dubbed the "King of the Delta Blues," lived a life that was shrouded in mystery. Some sources say he was born in Hazelhurst, Mississippi; others say Robinsville, Mississippi. Some believe he was about thirty years old when he came to San Antonio to record; others, including his producer, Don Law, remember him being only seventeen or eighteen. Photographs of him are as rare as good information. Few people disagree, however, on the talent Johnson possessed. He was a new kind of bluesman who could make his guitar scream to match his powerful voice.

Johnson came to San Antonio after meeting with Ernie Oertle, a talent scout for the American Record Corporation. Oertle cut a deal and sent the guitarist to the Alamo City to record for the recording company's Vocalion label. On November 23, 1936, he recorded eight songs, including "I Believe I'll Dust My Broom," which would later become a hit for Elmore James.

The next day Johnson disappeared. The country boy from Mississippi was obviously overwhelmed by the entertainment options a city the size of San Antonio offered. Nobody is quite sure what kind of trouble he got into, but Don Law had to make a trip down to the police department, where Johnson was being held on a vagrancy charge. On November 26 he resumed recording, laying down the tune "32:20 Blues." On the next day he put seven more songs to tape, including "Cross Road Blues," a song Eric Clapton and Cream later turned into a platinum record that would inspire the movie *Crossroads*. Because of the record's limited distribution (the songs were released only in the South to a predominantly black customer base), Johnson's vinyl offerings became instant collectors' items. Only one song, "Terraplane Blues," sold well to the general public.

In 1938 John Hammond, who became a music business legend for producing Bessie Smith, Benny Goodman, and Stevie Ray Vaughan, was planning his "Spiritual Swing" concert for Carnegie Hall. Hammond sought Law's help in locating Johnson, and Law discovered that Johnson had been poisoned to death under mysterious circumstances a few days earlier. A brilliant talent, and possibly a successful career, was tragically cut short. Details about the bluesman's life remain sketchy, but the recording sessions have become legendary.

3 Joske's

The San Antonio retail legend was started modestly in 1867 by Julius Joske in a one-room adobe building on Austin Street. An earlier effort to start a dry goods store failed, but on the second venture he had the help of his sons Siegfried, Albert, and Alexander. In 1875 a new store opened on Alamo Plaza with a new name, Joske Brothers. The store moved again in 1878, this time to its historic spot on Commerce and Alamo Streets. The new two-story outlet known as the Big Store was an immediate hit. In 1903 two more stories were added, as well as elevators. The first escalators in San Antonio were added in 1935—the same year Joske's became the first air-conditioned department store in Texas.

The store was famous for the big sign that hovered over Alamo Plaza for many years. Many remember the sign being atop Joske's, but actually it was atop the adjacent Conroy Building. The fifty-by-five-foot sign, famous for its giant cowboy roping a steer, was used to advertise a variety of businesses until Joske's bought the building and began using the sign exclusively.

Joske's eventually tore down the neighboring building, expanding in 1939 and 1953, until it took up virtually the

The funeral procession for Alexander Joske passes by his store, July 10, 1925.

whole block. One neighbor decided not to sell, so the department store just built around them. For years the German Catholic church that was surrounded on three sides by the new additions was known simply as St. Joske's. The new store was dubbed the largest store in the largest state (after Alaska was admitted to the Union, it became known as the *grandest* store in the *grandest* state). The big sign that was supposed to be re-erected atop the new store never returned due to structural problems. In 1942 the sign was donated to a wartime scrap metal drive.

The greatest time to visit the downtown store was during Christmas. It was then that the store set up its elaborate Fantasyland, entertained generations of the city's youngsters. Opening in 1960, it attracted over which a million visitors in its first five years. Talking Bears, the Magic Train, the Church of Every Faith, Santa's Castle, and the Fantasyland Town Square were featured. Outside, a giant Santa adorned the roof (during Easter, Peter Rabbit sat on the roof).

Joske's opened its first branch in 1957 at the Las Palmas Shopping Center (an H-E-B now occupies the site). Eventually, seven Joske's stores stretched across Texas. In 1987 the downtown store closed for remodeling. Rivercenter Mall was being built on the old parking lot, and they were preparing the store to be one of the anchor tenants. Unfortunately, Joske's never reopened. The Dillard department store chain bought out the seven outlets and announced plans to convert them into Dillard stores. Despite much outcry and pleading by conservationists, the Joske's name became history: the large letters on the corners of the building were removed and replaced with a Rivercenter sign. The biggest store in the biggest state became nothing more than a memory.

4 **Frost Brothers**

In 1917, the dry goods merchants Jonas and William Frost bought a dress store at 217 Houston. The Frost Brothers

Department Store catered to San Antonio's upper crust for many years. In 1949 the Art Deco outlet doubled in size when it expanded straight through to Travis Street. To get from the Men's Department on Travis Street to the Women's Department on Houston Street, patrons had to cross through an alley. Frost Brothers eventually had locations in North Star Mall, Crossroads Mall, and nine other locations throughout the state. The downtown store closed in 1987 for remodeling and vowed to reopen when construction on Houston Street was finished and the Majestic remodeling was complete. But it never did. In 1989 Frost Brothers announced it was going out of business. On June 29 the North Star Mall store closed, leaving San Antonio without a homegrown department store.

5 Grand Opera House

Located across from the Alamo, the Grand Opera House was once the site of the city's premier social events. Opening in 1886, the performing arts hall seated 1,500 in solid oak chairs with mohair upholstery. Designed by J. P. McElfatrick and Son of St. Louis, the Grand was considered one of the finest opera houses in the country. Its opening night featured Emma Abbott and Lucretia Borgia, two top performers of the time. The opera house had most of its success during its first two years. When motion pictures came into vogue, the Grand began showing films. Shortly after World War I, the Grand Opera House closed. The building was modified and became the H. L. Green variety store. Green's closed in the 1980s, and the building is now the home of a wax museum and a Ripley's Believe It or Not showcase.

6 Vance House

This colonial mansion was built by James Vance in 1859 on 210 E. Nueva. Vance, from Stebaune, Ireland, built one of San Antonio's finest homes for his bride, using lumber and wrought iron brought from New Orleans. A tank affixed to the roof made this one of the first buildings to offer the luxury of running water. The stately mansion was host to many dignitaries, including Robert E. Lee. In the 1930s the Department of the Interior's Historic Building Survey chose the Vance House as an outstanding architectural example. The house passed through various owners and was once home to the Texas State Employment Service. Torn down in the early 1950s, it was replaced with the new Federal Reserve Bank, and a plaque marks the site.

7 Playland Park

Two generations of San Antonians have fond memories of a small amusement park known as Playland Park. The fifteen-acre park was opened in 1941 by Jimmy Johnson, a former army soldier, who had the idea for a place where folks could gather for good clean fun when he was stationed at Fort Sam. Johnson first opened an amusement center on the polo field at Brackenridge Park, but in 1941 he moved it to the corner of N. Alamo and Broadway, which was one of the main thoroughfares into the city and quite a busy intersection. Johnson personally designed many of the rides and attractions at Playland Park. One of his favorites was something called "What Every Man Knows about Women." When parkgoers deposited ten cents, they got to peek inside and see nothing, and Johnson would enjoy a private laugh.

Some of the more popular rides included the Rocket Roller Coaster, the Transylvania Trolley, the Zoomer, and a 1917 carousel. However, Playland Park was more than rides. Johnson added other attractions, too, such as the Pleasant Valley Chapel, which provided a place for meditation. The paper-eating clowns with the vacuum mouths were a popular feature with young kids, who could not wait to throw away their soda cups and hot-dog wrappers. Mother Goose Land, the miniature Mount Rushmore, and the Liberty Bell Replica were just some of the special touches that Johnson added to make Playland Park a one-of-a-kind place.

In September 1980, the day after Labor Day, Johnson closed the doors forever, citing taxes and high utility rates for the park's demise. At the time it cost ten dollars to get into Astroworld and just twenty-five cents to get into Playland, but an advanced highway system meant that growing parks such as Astroworld and Six Flags were more accessible by car. When Jimmy Johnson closed Playland, he said, "It's like losing a child."

Many of the attractions were bought by other amusement parks. The roller coaster was moved to Pennsylvania, and the chapel was moved to the north side and converted into an Anglican Catholic church. In later years the old proprietor would charge five dollars to curiosity seekers who wanted to visit the park. Johnson often said, "When you retire, you die." The man who brought so many San Antonians thirty-nine years of good clean fun died three years later.

Nothing remains of Playland Park, but if you drive to the corner of Alamo and Broadway, you can still the remnants of the sign over the main gate.

8 HemisFair Arena

Built in 1968 for the World's Fair, HemisFair Arena was the original home of the San Antonio Spurs. The lower circular arena originally seated just under 11,000. It served the city well for over twenty-five years, hosting sporting events, circuses, and the likes of Frank Sinatra, Elvis (three times), Led Zeppelin, Van Halen, Diana Ross, and the Rolling Stones.

When the Spurs joined the NBA, the one-deck arena was the smallest in the league and inadequate for the crowds. In 1977 the city approved a plan to raise the roof and add a second deck of seats that would result in a new capacity of just over 16,000. Construction crews lifted the 5.5-ton roof thirty-three feet above the arena and filled in the open space with an upper deck.

The result was a quirky facility where posts obstructed views from the lower seating bowl. But the upper deck was right on top of the action, and provided a wonderful view of the court. The new configuration, combined with the notoriously rambunctious Spurs fans, created the loudest arena in the NBA. When the Spurs moved to the Alamodome, HemisFair Arena was used for concerts and a variety of other events. Despite the efforts of a local concert promoter to save the facility, HemisFair Arena was demolished in 1995, when the Convention Center needed to be expanded.

9   Peacock Military Academy

Professor Wesley Peacock moved to San Antonio to start a boarding school. Located near Woodlawn Lake, the Peacock School for Boys opened in 1894. The site was ideal for a boys' boarding school for two reasons: its proximity to one of the nation's largest military posts (Fort Sam Houston) and the city's growth, which provided an excellent economic base and rail transportation. Military training was added to the school in 1900, and a new building was erected on the grounds near West End Lake (as Woodlawn Lake was called back then).

In 1904 the school was chartered by the state of Texas and was one of the first three institutions recognized by the U.S. government. Enrollment peaked during the First World War, when army officers readied young men for military service. From 1920 to 1926 the school was used by the Veterans Bureau as a vocational training facility for ex-servicemen. In 1926 the school officially became the Peacock Military Academy and was run by Wesley Peacock's sons, Wesley Jr. and Donald Peacock. The academy became widely known for its excellent drill teams, who won much recognition for their precision, and for a football team that was once coached by a young army lieutenant named Dwight Eisenhower.

In 1973 the school closed its doors for good. The facility, consisting of fifteen buildings and twenty acres, was transferred to the Salvation Army.

10 The 12th Hole

After a full day of golf, linksters usually retire to the nineteenth hole for a few cool ones and a snack. But Brackenridge Golf Course had a different tradition. Ask any old-timer about the 12th Hole, and he will tell you about the best burgers and the coldest beer this side of Augusta.

For many years, just beyond the twelfth green at Brack was a small privately owned snack bar called the 12th Hole that sold whatever a golfer required, as long as it could be cooked on a grill or kept in a cooler. It was the perfect way to beat the heat. Golfing parties would play twelve holes, then stop and refresh themselves before finishing the final six holes.

When McAllister Freeway was built, it cut severely into the Brackenridge course, which had to be reshaped, making it much smaller. The twelfth green was on the other side of the freeway, leaving it and the restaurant completely cut off from the course.

The 12th Hole restaurant tried to make it on its own, but it was difficult to reach. It passed through different owners and finally closed in 1985. If you take Terry Court off N. St. Mary's Street, near the Ashby/St. Mary's intersection, you can find the overgrown green. Just a few feet from the green under the old pecan tree and overgrown vines is the remains of the 12th Hole.

11 Whopper Burger

This local hamburger fast food chain set the standard for San Antonians for decades. Fred M. Bates opened the first Whopper Burger in 1955. There was not a neighborhood in San Antonio that did not have a Whopper Burger. Some came for the crinkle fries, and others stopped for the Orange Freeze. No two Whopper Burger buildings were the same. Some were modern, with slick clean lines, some featured Googie architecture, and some featured the outdated, robust Whopper Boy logo.

Because the local chain held the rights to the term "Whopper," Burger King was unable to open restaurants in San Antonio. In 1986 the Pillsbury Company (which then owned the national chain) bought out Whopper Burger from Bates's widow, and the home of the original whopper was gone. Some of the locations closed, others became used car lots, and some were transformed into Burger Kings. Many simply changed names and little else. Of those that simply changed their name, only two remain: Murf's Better Burger on West Avenue and Burger Boy on St. Mary's (which still features the Orange Freeze!).

12 Brackenridge Park Sky Ride

For over thirty years San Antonians could get a unique view of the city from a gondola high above Brackenridge Park. The park's sky ride, built by Von Roll Tramways of New York, opened in 1964 at a cost of $300,000 and rose a hundred feet above the Sunken Gardens before dropping passengers off near the zoo. For fifty cents, a rider got a round-trip ticket back across the garden. In 1999 the sky ride came to an end. It had fallen into disrepair and would have cost the city millions to fix. Instead, the park chose to remove the ride three years later. The brightly colored gondolas were auctioned off for $1,000 each.

Four Favorite San Antonio Places Brought Back

1 San Pedro Springs Pool

San Pedro Park is one of the oldest parks in the United States, having been set aside in 1729 as public land by King Philip V of Spain. The attraction was the headwaters of San Pedro Creek. In 1922 the city built its first public pool at the park, with water from the springs flushing out the pool every eight

The old Brackenridge Park Sky Ride.

hours. By the 1940s the city's water demand had decreased the water flow to the point that the pool couldn't stay clean. It was closed for over ten years and replaced with a more modern chlorinated fenced-in pool in 1954 with the financial help of grocer Howard E. Butt.

In 2000 the pool was rebuilt in the shape of the original lake. The cypress trees that once lined the old pool encircle its replacement. The new pool has the look and feel of the original, and during heavy rains, the springs flow as before.

2 Esquire Bar

The Esquire is the oldest bar on the River Walk and, in fact, actually predates it. Opened in 1933 to celebrate the end of Prohibition, the Esquire was known for having the longest bar, which was almost as long as the establishment itself, stretching from Commerce Street to the San Antonio River behind the building.

In 2006 the Esquire closed just before the city was about to shut it down as a nuisance. A large crowd gathered on its last night, including Chris Hill, who bought the building in 2008 with plans to find someone to lease and operate the Esquire. In 2011 Hill, a self-proclaimed reluctant restaurateur, restored the Esquire—even reproducing the original tobacco-darkened wallpaper—and reopened the bar himself, making food available for the first time. When he opened the bar, the first patron was an old regular who said, "Hell, it doesn't look like you've done a whole lot." Today the Esquire has a rather upscale appearance.

3 Cool Crest Miniature Golf

Cool Crest, the oldest miniature golf course in San Antonio, opened in 1929 on Fredericksburg Road. In 1937 Harold Metzger and his wife, Maria, leased the land and improved it, which included the addition of a second course (still dubbed the "New Course") in 1957. Generations of San Antonians flocked to the imaginative mini-golf park, with its lush banana

The Hays Street Bridge.

plants and tropical feel. In 2007, seventy years after her husband took it over, Maria Metzger closed Cool Crest, as she became too old to operate it. She died in 2010, and Cool Crest fell into disrepair. In 2013 the Andry family bought it, and the course was reopened on June 30, bringing back the self-proclaimed "World's Finest" miniature golf course for future generations.

4 Hays Street Bridge

In the early part of the twentieth century, the Galveston, Harrisburg, and San Antonio Railroad wanted to build train tracks on the east side of the city. Knowing this would block access to downtown for citizens on Dignowity Hill, the city required the railroad to build the Hays Street Bridge over the tracks. The structure used materials from two other bridges, both constructed in 1881, and moved to San Antonio in 1910. If you look closely, you can see the two distinct spans on the trusses that make up the Hays Street Bridge.

By 1982 it had deteriorated to the point that it could no longer accommodate automobile traffic. The bridge sat barricaded for twenty-eight years until it was renovated and reopened in 2010 as a bike and pedestrian bridge, thanks to the efforts of a variety of private and public groups. The Hays Street Bridge is now on the National Register of Historic Places.

Six San Antonio Projects That Never Became Reality

1 Alamo monument

In 1912 the Alamo Heroes Monument Association was chartered, with the goal to erect a monument in Alamo Plaza in honor of those who lost their lives in the battle. The AHMA supported a plan by architect Alfred Giles to build an 802-foot tower, which would have cost $2 million. The tower would be surrounded by thirty-foot-tall statues of Alamo heroes and would have four elevators to take sightseers to the top, where they would be able to see for a hundred miles. The lower levels would be filled with museums, galleries, and a library. Because of the cost of the project and its dimensions (it would have dwarfed the Alamo and everything else downtown), enthusiasm for the project diminished.

2 Boardwalk and Baseball

When Sea World of Texas was built in 1986, there were plans for an adjacent amusement park dubbed Boardwalk and Baseball, modeled after a park in Florida, also owned by Sea World's parent company, HB&J. Unlike Sea World, the new park would feature a variety of rides, including roller coasters, and possibly a baseball stadium. Then Opryland USA announced its intention to build a similar theme park in north San Antonio. Plans for Boardwalk and Baseball were indefinitely postponed when HB&J sold Sea World to Anheuser Busch. Coincidently, Opryland never built their project either.

3 A 60,000-seat Alamo Stadium

When Clinton Manges was awarded the San Antonio franchise in the United States Football League, he announced his intention to expand the high school stadium to 60,000 seats by 1986. This would have given the city a facility that was capable of hosting major league attractions and also met conditions set by the new league. Manges backed up his promise by signing a thirty-year lease and two ten-year options. He did give the stadium a new track, an Astroturf field, and a fresh coat of paint in the team's colors, but that was the extent of the improvements. Unfortunately for the city, he could barely afford to pay his players, much less expand the stadium's capacity. The league and the team folded in 1986, leaving Alamo Stadium virtually unchanged until a renovation in 2014.

4 University of Texas at San Antonio at Hemisfair Plaza

After HemisFair '68 many considered the ninety-two-acre tract an ideal place for the new university. The campus would have been centrally located, so that all would have equal access to the facility. It would also play an important role in the revitalization of downtown. However, the UT Board of Regents rejected downtown in favor of donated land on the far north side. The land (donated by people who had vast land holdings in the area and would benefit from development) effectively made the new school a commuter campus. The HemisFair site sat vacant for twenty years until the grounds were redeveloped into a park for $133 million. A downtown UTSA satellite campus was finally built thirty years after the fair.

5 Centennial Exposition

Competition for the 1936 Texas Centennial Exposition was fierce. San Antonio put in its own bid to host the state's hundredth anniversary by proposing to build a fairground on the city's east side near Freeman Coliseum. A street in the area was named Exposition Avenue in anticipation of the event. The exposition was eventually awarded to Dallas, which held the festivities at the state fair site. As for Exposition Avenue, it was renamed Coca-Cola Boulevard for the nearby bottling plant.

6 Bowen's Island skyscrapers, aka San Antonio's Rockefeller Center

When the Smith-Young Tower (now the Tower Life Building) opened in June 1929, it was not only the city's tallest building but also the first of a series of proposed skyscrapers that were to rival New York's Rockefeller Center. The collection of buildings was to stretch for four city blocks on a peninsula of the river known as Bowen's Island. A few months after the grand opening, the stock market crashed and the Great Depression began. The company that owned the Smith-Young Tower dissolved within ten years, and the building went into receivership. Plans to build San Antonio's Rockefeller Center never materialized.

San Antonio's Most Influential Architects

Texas Architecture magazine listed the following (with the exception of Alfred Giles, Henry Muñoz, and Lake/Flato) among Texas's most influential architects.

O'Neil Ford

O'Neil Ford's mark is left on every corner of San Antonio. Perhaps the city's most famous designer, Ford never had the benefit of a formal education. With only two years of undergraduate work at North Texas Teachers College (now the University of North Texas) and a basic architecture course from the International Correspondence School of Scranton, Pennsylvania, he entered the office of Dallas architect David R. Williams as an apprentice. Williams served as his first role model, and together they designed homes throughout Texas.

When Williams was appointed administrator of the National Youth Administration in 1936, he was able to direct commissions to Ford, the first being the Little Chapel of the Woods on the campus of Texas Women's University in Denton. The young designer came to San Antonio as a consulting designer in the restoration of La Villita, another NYA project.

Over the years, Ford has designed some of the city's biggest projects, including portions of Trinity University, the first phase of UTSA, and the Tower of the Americas. Ford also submitted a plan for Hemisfair Plaza that would have incorporated more of the historic buildings into the fair site, but it was rejected.

Ford was appointed to the National Council of the Arts in 1968 by Lyndon Johnson and to the American Council for

Arts in Education in 1975 by David Rockefeller. The first endowed chair in the School of Architecture at the University of Texas was named for Ford. A small plaza in La Villita behind the Little Church was also named in his honor. He died in 1982.

Atlee B. and Robert M. Ayres

Atlee Ayres founded his firm in 1900 and was joined by his son in 1924. Together they designed some of San Antonio's most impressive projects, including the complex on the corner of Villita and St. Mary's Streets (which entailed the city's first skyscraper), the Smith-Young Tower (now the Tower Life Building), the Federal Reserve Bank (now the Mexican Consulate), and the Plaza Hotel (now Granada Homes). This complex, built right before the Depression, was one of the biggest undertakings of its time. Its owner wanted it to be the new center of downtown.

Another structure designed by the pair was the City Central Bank and Trust Building (now the South Texas Building) on the corner of Navarro and Houston Streets. When it was constructed in 1919, it was the costliest bank building in Texas and the tallest in the city—thus its nickname, the Million Dollar Bank.

Ayres and Ayres were also responsible for the YWCA (now DPT Laboratories), the old City Public Service Building, the administration building on Randolph Air Force Base (better known as Taj Mahal), and the Municipal Auditorium. They also designed the Atkinson home, which is now the McNay Art Museum.

An office building at the corner of Travis and Broadway was built in 1911 and renamed on April 17, 1985, in honor of its architect, who had his offices there until 1928. Ayres also designed the adjacent Moore building (now 110 Broadway) and was the state architect of Texas in 1915. Ayres and Ayres was always a small firm and closed in 1977 with the death of son Robert Ayres.

Alfred Giles

Born in England, Alfred Giles chose San Antonio as his home in 1873. He designed courthouse buildings throughout South Texas and numerous buildings in San Antonio, and his mark is still evident in the city over 100 years later.

Some of the city's most prominent structures owe their existence to Giles—the Bexar County Courthouse, the Fort Sam Infantry Post barracks, the Mother House at Incarnate Word College, the Menger Hotel, the Crockett building on Alamo Plaza, and the old Bexar County Jail on Camaron Street. Like many prominent architects, Giles began by designing homes. He built many of the mansions in the King William district, including the Steves Homestead and the Groos House. His firm also drew up the plans for Lambermont and the commander's house at Fort Sam Houston.

Many of his architectural gems have been lost over the years, such as Haymarket Plaza, the original Joske's Brothers store, the Groos Bank, and the first Brackenridge High School. Luckily, a majority of his work has been saved and renovated in San Antonio, and very few South Texas counties are without a Giles courthouse.

Carleton Adams

Carleton Adams and his uncle, Carl C. Adams, founded and operated the city's leading commercial architecture firm from the 1910s to the 1950s. Adams's most famous work was Jefferson High School, which was featured in *Life* magazine in 1937 as the country's most outstanding modern school. Adams was also responsible for the design of the Alamo Cenotaph, which featured sculptures by Pompeo Coppini.

Adams and Adams designed the San Antonio Drug Company's offices on the corner of St. Mary's and Market Streets, the Great American Life Insurance Building, and the National Bank of Commerce. Perhaps his most prestigious work was the Hall of State in Dallas Fair Park for the Texas

Centennial in 1936. Adams also designed the student union at Texas A&M University.

Ralph Cameron

Ralph Cameron began working as a draftsman for Alfred Giles at age thirteen and later worked for Adams and Adams in 1912. He opened his own office in 1914. Cameron's best works are within blocks of each other. He was the supervising architect of the Scottish Rite Temple in 1924, and he also collaborated on the post office and U.S. courthouse in Alamo Plaza. The Medical Arts Building (now the Alamo Plaza Hotel) across the street was also his design. The architect was responsible for several homes in Monte Vista and Olmos Park, including the Hornaday and Spencer residences.

Robert Hugman

A San Antonio native, Robert Hugman envisioned a developed river walk that he wanted to call the "Shops of Aragon and Romula." However, in the late 1920s such a plan was not popular, and many wanted simply to pave over the river to prevent flooding. But Hugman persevered and was the architect for the River Walk until he had a fight with city hall, when he was relieved of his duties right before its completion. Hugman finished his career as an employee of Randolph Air Force Base. He took great pride in the development of the River Walk, especially after HemisFair, when his vision grew into reality. The bells at Arneson River Theatre were dedicated on November 1, 1978, in honor of his service to the city.

Bartlett Cocke

Bartlett Cocke returned to his hometown of San Antonio in 1924, after graduating from MIT's School of Architecture. He began as an apprentice for the Kellwood Company and opened his own office in 1927. During the Depression, he was the deputy director of the Historic American Building Survey, producing drawings of several pre–Civil War Texas structures.

His first major project came in 1938, when he beat out Ralph Cameron and Ayres & Ayres to design the Joske's building (now Rivercenter Mall) for Alamo Plaza. Cocke traveled across the country, visiting fifty-seven department stores before drawing up plans for the critically acclaimed building. He went on to design many office buildings, malls, and public schools, including a joint venture with O'Neil Ford to build Trinity University and UTSA.

Cocke was the first University of Texas alum to be honored with a professorship in his name. He also served as the president of the Texas Society of Architects in 1944 and 1945.

George Willis

When George Willis first arrived in San Antonio at the age of thirty-one, he worked for Atlee B. Ayres. Having worked as a draftsman for Frank Lloyd Wright and with a number of Prairie School practitioners, he was one of the most learned architects in Texas when he opened his own firm in 1917.

Willis's Milam Building was the tallest reinforced concrete building in the world in 1928—and the first to be air-conditioned. He designed the addition to the Bexar County Courthouse and the Sunken Garden Theater, and he worked with Emmett T. Jackson and Ayres & Ayres to build the Municipal Auditorium.

Henry J. Steinbomer

A man of strong faith, Henry Steinbomer was Texas's premier church architect in the 1940s and 1950s. He cofounded the Historic Buildings Foundation and worked with sculptor Gutzon Borglum and Clara Driscoll in persuading the city to preserve the Alamo. He also worked with Bartlett Cocke and Fred Buenz to save several historic homes now on the grounds of the Witte Museum.

Steinbomer's first church project was an education building for Alamo Heights Methodist Church. He later planned the chapel and several additions to the grounds. Between

World War II and 1964 he designed over 75 church projects in San Antonio and over 150 in South Texas, including the Travis Park Methodist Youth Building, St. Luke's Episcopal Church, and Jefferson Methodist Church.

Andrew Pérez III

Andrew Pérez was a disciple of O'Neil Ford's, working with him from 1966 to 1970. He has designed several houses, schools, banks, and office buildings throughout South Texas. His most noted work came in 1982, during the battle over the Texas Theatre, when he was appointed by Mayor Cisneros to head a task force on historic preservation. The committee registered over a thousand historic buildings and wrote a nationally acclaimed historic preservation ordinance that was adopted by the city council in 1987. Pérez took over as the head of the School of Architecture at UTSA in 1987 and retired from teaching in 2011.

Lake/Flato

David Lake and Ted Flato met as young architects in the offices of O'Neil Ford. In 1984 the two started their own firm with a commitment to architecture that connected to the environment. They have helped reshape San Antonio with the redevelopment of the Pearl Brewery, the redesign of Main Plaza and its connection to the River Walk, and the AT&T Center. Winners of numerous national and international awards, their work and their distinct style spans the globe.

Muñoz and Company (formerly Kell Muñoz Architects)

Henry Muñoz's firm traces its heritage to Bartlett Cocke and the office he opened with John Kell Sr. in 1927. The firm's projects include the restoration of Our Lady of the Lake University's main building (after fire gutted it in 2008), the redesigned Henry B. González Convention Center, and the campus of Texas A&M University–San Antonio. Also in its portfolio is the Mission Branch Library, which occupies the site of the former Mission Drive-in Theater, so named for nearby Mission San José. Oddly enough, despite being the firm's namesake, Muñoz is not an architect by training.

Seven Stories about San Antonio Art and Artists

1 Gutzon Borglum and Mount Rushmore

One of the most intriguing artists to pass through San Antonio was noted sculptor Gutzon Borglum, who came to the city in 1925 to create a memorial for the Trail Drivers Museum. He immediately won the respect of Texans, who treated him as the ultimate celebrity when he toured the state with a model of his creation.

Borglum was an avowed anti-Semite and often spoke against the so-called Jewish Establishment and their control of the banking industry. However, many of his patrons, financial backers, and close friends were Jewish, including Supreme Court Justice Felix Frankfurter, who, like many of his contemporaries, accepted the self-proclaimed anti-Semite as a valued friend who was uncompromising in his beliefs. When Hitler began exterminating Jews, Borglum, the man of many contradictions, became his outspoken opponent. One of Hitler's first acts upon invading Poland was to destroy Borglum's statue of Woodrow Wilson.

Politically active, the artist allowed Czechoslovakian rebels to train on his Connecticut estate during World War I. Also, during the war he investigated the aircraft industry for corruption. He was an advisor to presidents and chiefs of state, and he became a powerful member of the Ku Klux Klan when the racist organization was trying to mainstream its cause.

When Borglum arrived in San Antonio, he had just been fired by the group who had commissioned him to create a monument in Stone Mountain, Georgia, honoring

The Alamo Heights bus shelter made by Dionicio Rodríguez, 1929.

Confederate heroes. He left Georgia a fugitive for destroying a vital model of the uncompleted sculpture. Borglum stayed in the city for many years, working out of his Mill Race Studio in Brackenridge Park, which he had modified from a former water works facility. Borglum created many famous pieces here, including his statue of Woodrow Wilson for the Polish government. And it was here that Borglum designed his greatest and most famous work of art—a giant carving of four ex-presidents on Mount Rushmore. He lived in San Antonio when he wasn't supervising the work in South Dakota.

Borglum left a large legacy. His art is displayed in the White House and the New York Metropolitan Museum of Art, as well as in Los Angeles, Detroit, Newark, Chicago, and San Antonio. He designed the flame in the Statue of Liberty's torch. As the head of the Texas Beautification Plan he proposed ideas, such as a Corpus Christi waterfront, that were years ahead of their time. As for San Antonio, his contributions to the city are mostly forgotten. He left for California in the 1930s after losing out on the Alamo Cenotaph commission.

His studio was turned over to the San Antonio Art League, which used it for young artists for many years. But at some point, the building was abandoned and sat in quiet ruins, adjacent to the Brackenridge Golf Course parking lot.

2 Dionicio Rodríguez, San Antonio's most accessible artist

Thousands of San Antonians who have caught the bus on Broadway near the Alamo Heights Central Market grocery store have sat in a peculiar bus stop that appears to be made of petrified wood. But few know the story behind the unique piece of faux bois artwork and the man who made it. Dionicio Rodríguez created the city's most accessible work of art at the corner of Broadway and Patterson in 1931. The bus shelter was donated to the city of Alamo Heights by the Alamo Cement company and has only been moved once, a few feet, when the street was paved.

Many believe that the shelter is made of petrified wood. Actually it's made of cement, Rodríguez's chosen medium. The artist, who was born in Mexico City in 1891, learned the unusual art form from a Spanish national who showed him a unique chemical process to make cement look like petrified wood. One of Rodríguez's earliest patrons was Dr. Aureliano Urrutia, who introduced him to Charles Baumberger Sr., founder of Alamo Cement.

Baumberger commissioned several pieces, including the Alamo Heights shelter, a fish pond at the cement plant, and a unique fence at the Alamo Cement headquarters. The old plant office has been redeveloped into the Stone Werks restaurant, where patrons can now enjoy the work that was hidden for years.

A bridge near Brackenridge Park's headquarters and an old entrance to the Sunken Gardens were both Rodriguez's creations. The gate to Sunken Gardens reads "Chinese Tea Gardens" rather than Japanese Sunken Gardens because the entryway was made during World War II when anti-Japanese sentiment was high, and the name of the gardens was changed. Other examples of his work can be found at private residences throughout the city, as well as in Memphis, Little Rock, New York City, Chattanooga, Cuba, and Mexico.

Rodríguez was very secretive about the chemical process he used and preferred local cement because it contained no sand or mortar. He used simple tools such as a fork, knife, and spoon to shape his creations.

Rodríguez died in San Antonio in 1955, leaving his protégé and great-nephew, Carlos Cortés, to continue his faux bois artwork, which you can find at the grotto on the Museum Reach extension of the River Walk.

3   Pompeo Coppini and the Alamo Cenotaph

Situated on the north side of Alamo Plaza, the Alamo Cenotaph has received worldwide acclaim. The cenotaph honors the fallen heroes of the Alamo, whose remains are elsewhere. The monument has a base made of Texas pink granite and a shaft constructed of Georgia gray marble that rises sixty feet. The title of the work is *The Spirit of Sacrifice*. On the south and north sides are feminine figures who symbolize Texas and the United States. On the east and west sides are depictions of James Bowie, James Bonham, Davy Crockett, and William Travis, who represent those who died during the battle.

The cenotaph cost $100,000 and was the creation of renowned Italian sculptor Pompeo Coppini, who was born in Italy and studied at the Accademia di Belle Arte in Florence. The sculptor moved to America in 1896 and became a naturalized American citizen in 1902. He eventually established a home and a studio in San Antonio because it reminded him of the terrain of his native Tuscany. Throughout his lifetime, he created monuments all over Texas, such as the five statues that comprise the Confederate Monument on the grounds of the state capitol.

Other works include the monument at Sam Houston's tomb in Huntsville, a memorial to Governor Sul Ross at Texas A&M, and the *Come and Take It* memorial in Gonzales. Just blocks from the Cenotaph are two more of his works, the front door of the Scottish Rite Temple and the sculpture over the entrance of the *Express-News* building. Coppini headed the art department at Trinity from 1942 until 1945, when he moved to New York. Coppini died in 1957 and was buried in San Antonio.

4 Bob "Daddy-O" Wade and the giant boots

Arguably San Antonio's most famous piece of art sits on Loop 410 in front of North Star Mall. The World's Largest Pair of Boots has been in countless postcards, photographs, and commercials. The boots were created by artist Bob "Daddy-O" Wade in 1979 for the Washington Project for the Arts. The large-scale work of public art was constructed and displayed just a few blocks from the White House for over a year on Twelfth Street and Avenue G. After the exhibit was over, the Rouse Corporation offered to buy the boots to place outside North Star Mall.

The transportation of the giant boots was an adventure in itself. They got stuck in an overpass before leaving the city, and the trucks transporting them had to take back roads all the way to Texas to avoid police, using CB radios to alert the drivers to possible trouble.

In the early days at the mall, KTSA radio became the talk of the town when they built a broadcast booth atop the boots. For a short time, a homeless man made a home inside. Today the World's Largest Pair of Boots is one of San Antonio's most recognizable sites.

Another piece of Wade's art sits on the south side, off 1201 Somerset Road, where a full-size Plymouth Fury has been made into a giant junkyard dog. Wade made it for a car enthusiast friend who owned the salvage yard. A deal was struck: the work of art in exchange for the restoration of Wade's '57 Chevy.

5 Jesse Treviño and La Veladora of Our Lady of Guadalupe

The world's largest mosaic of Our Lady of Guadalupe sits on the west side at 1301 Guadalupe Street. The forty-foot candle's flame is a memorial to 9/11 victims. Jesse Treviño is a noted artist in San Antonio whose other works include *The Spirit of Healing*, a nine-story-high mural on the southern wall of Santa Rosa Hospital that features 150,000 hand-cut tiles. The model for the child in the piece was Treviño's son.

Treviño is a Vietnam veteran and Purple Heart recipient who lost his right arm in the war. When he returned, he enrolled in San Antonio College, where he learned to use his left hand to create. He earned an art degree at Our Lady of the

Lake University. His first mural, *La historia chicana*, is on display in the university's Sueltenfuss Library.

6   Eugene O. Goldbeck

San Antonio's most industrious and famous photographer, Eugene Goldbeck, traveled the globe for over eighty years. Born in San Antonio in 1891 (or 1892, as his alternate birth certificate indicates), Goldbeck was bitten by the photo bug at an early age. By nine years old, his portfolio included a shot of President William McKinley, an extraordinary feat considering photography was still in its infancy. By age fifteen he was selling photos of his classmates at school and soon began supplying photographs to both the *San Antonio Light* and the *Express-News*.

In 1910 Goldbeck graduated from Main Avenue High School and began working as a full-time photographer. His skill with the camera was recognized throughout town. When Lieutenant Benjamin Delahauf Foulois made the military's first flight on the parade ground at Fort Sam Houston, Goldbeck was there to record the event.

Two years later he purchased his first Cirkut panoramic camera and immediately began experimenting with this new technology. In fact, he set such a high standard for panoramic photography that his work is instantly recognized. One of his earliest shots is of the U.S. Army's entire air force in flight—a total of three planes. During World War I, Goldbeck joined the Photo Division of the U.S. Signal Corps and made ties with the military that would last a lifetime.

After the war Goldbeck returned to San Antonio. He later formed the National Photo and News Service in a two-story building in his backyard on the south side. The city was only a base of operations, though, because Goldbeck was a traveler. He shot photos in Japan, the Soviet Union, Egypt, the South Pacific, and many more places. The photographer lived into his nineties. In his final years he sold autographed photos for twenty-five dollars. Today a signed Goldbeck is virtually priceless.

7 The disappearing three-ton sculpture

Because art is in the eyes of the beholder, some works of art have been mistaken for junk. Such was the case for *Asteriskos,* a three-ton black metal sculpture by New Yorker Tony Smith that the Catto family commissioned for HemisFair. Its original location was between the Arena and the Convention Center. After the fair closed, the huge work disappeared, and it took over a year to find it. Unfortunately, it was no longer intact. It was apparently carted off, blow-torched into smaller pieces, fitted with wooden lids, and turned into tool boxes and ice chests for after-work beer parties at the Zarzamora Street Public Works Department yard. The Catto family commissioned a replica from the artist and donated it to the McNay Art Institute, where it sits today.

Seven Unique San Antonio Sports Stories

1 Dwight Eisenhower, head coach of the St. Mary's football team

Dwight Eisenhower played football as a youngster in Kansas and became a football star at West Point. In 1912 he was a running back on an army team that included Omar Bradley. Nicknamed the "Kansas Cyclone," Eisenhower was called one of the most promising backs in the East by a *New York Times* correspondent. An injury during a game against Tufts ended Eisenhower's football career at the academy during his freshman year.

After graduation in 1915, the newly commissioned lieutenant received orders to report to Fort Sam Houston. During the fall of that year, Eisenhower was approached by Peacock

Military Academy to coach its football team. The school offered him $150 for the season, a tidy sum compared to a lieutenant's pay. At first he refused because he felt that as an army officer, he would have no time for football. But the head of the academy was a friend of post commander General Frank Funston, who asked Eisenhower to accept the position, citing its benefit for the army. The new coach delivered a winning season for the 1915 Peacock Military Academy football team. A *San Antonio Express* correspondent wrote, "Those who have seen this officer operate with a football squad believe him to be one of the best coaches in Texas—bar none."

By 1916 Eisenhower was married, and Peacock had acquired a new coach. St. Louis College (now St. Mary's University) sought the winning coach for its team, which was dreadful. Coached by a group of priests, the team had not won a game in five years, and lopsided scores such as 50–0 were common. Under Eisenhower the small squad tied its first game, then went on to win five in a row. Although St. Louis lost its last game, it finished the season with a solid record of 5–1–1. Present at every game was the coach's young wife, Mamie, who was the only woman ever to receive a St. Louis or St. Mary's football letter. Quarterback Jim Sweeney told the *Express,* "We thought more of him than we did of any other coach we ever had. We respected him from the time he showed up until he left, and we fought as much for Mamie and the Douds (her parents who also attended the games) as we did the school. He was very frank and honest and we learned more about honor and discipline from him than we did anywhere else."

The priests at the college were so pleased with the season that they gave the coach and Mamie a victory dinner, and a long-lasting relationship between the school and the Eisenhowers developed. The president last visited the school in 1962 to talk to students and faculty. In 1987 his grandson, David Eisenhower, discussed his grandfather's connection to the university during the school's annual President's Dinner.

Eisenhower also spent some time coaching the school's baseball team. Ernest Stecker recalled to the *Express* in 1956 how he'd incurred the wrath of Coach Eisenhower during a close game. St. Louis was behind by one run with two men on, and the team's slugger was in the on-deck circle. Eisenhower signaled Stecker to bunt, but on the next pitch, Stecker slammed the ball for a triple. Instead of congratulations, all he received was a stern look. He had disobeyed orders.

2 St. Mary's football, 1930s powerhouse

St. Mary's University no longer has a football team, but for many years, the school had a prominent gridiron history. Probably its most successful period was in the 1930s, when Mose Simms was the athletic director and lifeblood of the team. Simms put up the money for the team and received a portion of the profits. He scoured the state for the best players, promising them a room, education, travel, and all the food they could eat. *Life* magazine ran a feature on him and St. Mary's recruiting efforts on October 16, 1939. The magazine showed the school's legendary double-decker blue bus, which logged an average of 10,000 miles a year, and stated that the school was "well on its way to becoming a football power."

Former *Houston Post* sports editor Clark Nealon, who once covered the school for the *San Antonio Light,* stated that Simms was the best promoter he ever saw: "Compared to him, Roy Hofheinz and Bud Adams are two-bit promoters." One of his greatest stunts was against San Francisco in 1936. Simms had the team practice in old tattered uniforms and stumble around during drills, which caused hoots and howls from opposing fans and players. Then on game day, the team took the field in brand-new uniforms. The home team quickly realized they had been duped.

Herman Richter of the old Richter's Bakery was a player on Simms's team in the late 1930s. Richter was the only player on the team who was not on scholarship. According to the now prominent businessman, most of the players that

Simms recruited were older students (some were even bald), who for some reason or another had dropped out of other schools. Very few were typical student athletes; most came only to play football. During one road trip, the Christian Brothers came to teach the players their lessons. When one reporter came to take a picture of the players studying, some of the so-called student athletes had to grab phone directories because they had not brought any books.

St. Mary's football was discontinued prior to World War II because the school had issues with Simms and shut down his traveling road show for good.

3 How San Antonio got the Spurs

In 1967 the Dallas Chaparrals were one of the founding teams of the upstart American Basketball Association. The team had never drawn well, averaging fewer than 3,000 fans a night. By 1973 the owners were desperately looking for a buyer and offered San Antonians Red McCombs and Angelo Drossos a unique deal: they could bring the team to San Antonio, lease it for two years, and then buy the team outright for two payments of $800,000.

The team, renamed the Spurs, had its own attendance woes until the arrival of a skinny young player named George Gervin. With Gervin, the team quickly improved, and attendance rocketed by the middle of the first season. Drossos then contacted the Dallas owners with a bit of a bluff. He told them he had run out of capital and they could have the team back, but the owners didn't want them back. So they struck a new deal. San Antonio could have the entire team immediately for one payment of $800,000.

Now in the NBA, the Spurs won their fifth championship in 2014.

4 Minor league stadium hosts major league stars

Organized baseball began in the 1890s, and San Antonio has always had a rich baseball history. Its heyday might have been in the '40s and '50s when the local nine played in Mission Stadium. Many proclaimed it the finest minor league stadium of its time. Sadly, when the team became an affiliate of the Houston Astros in the 1960s, owner Judge Roy Hofheinz disbanded the team and let the stadium fall into disrepair. Some said he feared it competing with his major league team.

Despite offers from local businessmen, Hofheinz refused to sell. The stadium sat vacant until 1973, when it was sold and torn down. The site is now home to Bexar County's juvenile detention center.

Many major league teams also held spring training here during the '20s and '30s. When native Texan Rogers Hornsby managed the Cardinals, he brought them here for training because he felt the San Antonio spring climate best matched the St. Louis summer climate, not to mention the fact that he enjoyed the hot springs at Terrell Wells. The Cardinals went on to win their first-ever world championship that season in 1926. The Cincinnati Reds also once trained at the Hot Wells Hotel.

Babe Ruth and the Yankees made a stop in San Antonio on March 31, 1931, playing an exhibition game in League Park (just north of the Pearl Brewery on Josephine Street). The Yankees beat the minor league San Antonio Indians 14–4 and stayed at the Menger Hotel during their visit. The Brooklyn Dodgers also barnstormed through the city. Both teams had their visits documented by noted San Antonio photographer E. O. Goldbeck during their stops.

5 The first Alamo Bowl

With the opening of the Alamodome in 1993, San Antonio became the host of a major college bowl game. But few realize that the Alamo Bowl pre-dates the domed stadium by forty-six years.

The year was 1947. The first-ever Alamo Bowl took place in Alamo Stadium. The event was sponsored by the Elks Club, who hoped to raise money for the Crippled Children's Hospital in Ottine. The New Year's Day game was to feature the Hardin-Simmons Cowboys, champions of the Border Conference (with an 11–0 record), against the co-champions of the Big Seven Conference, the University of Denver Pioneers (5–4–1). (The University of Denver tied with Utah State, who went to Fresno for the Raisin Bowl.) The Cowboys were 11-point favorites.

The game met with several difficulties. The day before the contest, San Antonio was hit by its worst ice storm in a hundred years. It was the most prolonged freeze since the 1800s. The police would not allow people to enter the stadium because the steps were dangerously slippery. The playing field was in equally poor shape, being covered by two inches of ice. The game had to be postponed from Wednesday, January 1, to Saturday, January 4. Both teams had to stay around town for the contest. Hardin-Simmons worked out at Alamo Heights Stadium, and Denver practiced at Harlandale Stadium.

When Saturday rolled around, the weather had not improved much, which really hurt attendance. A mere 3,730 fans witnessed Hardin-Simmons roll over Denver 20–0. The closest Denver got to the end zone was late in the fourth quarter, when they worked the ball to the five but lost it on downs.

Few sports fans recall the football events of that day. Most of the city was abuzz with the state basketball tournament game between Jefferson and Brackenridge high schools. The Elks Club wound up losing a substantial amount of money on the contest. And so, until 1993, the Alamo Bowl faded into obscurity along with the Oil Bowl, the Cigar Bowl, and the Raisin Bowl.

6   San Antonio's Cotton Bowl team

Next time you're bellied up to the bar at the Esquire, challenge the crowd to this simple question. The odds are in your favor that someone will owe you a cold one.

Q: Who is the only team from San Antonio to appear in the Cotton Bowl?

A: The Randolph Field Ramblers

Never heard of them? Few people have. The year was 1943, and World War II was in full swing. Many military posts had athletic teams filled with professional athletes and ex-college greats. Randolph Field was no exception. The Ramblers were stocked with many players who had already used up their college eligibility.

The team was led by former Tulsa All-American quarterback Glenn Dobbs (who also played for the professional Chicago Cardinals before the war). One of Dobbs's favorite receivers was player-coach Major Raymond Morse, who had played college ball for Oregon nine years earlier and also had some pro experience. And playing on the line for Randolph was Martin Ruby, who had been rated the best lineman two years earlier in the Southwest Conference while playing for A&M. Lieutenant Frank Tritic coached, and their trainer was Bibb A. Falk (as in UT's Disch-Falk Field), a former coach and baseball legend from the University of Texas.

The team was picked to face Texas in the 1944 New Year's Day Cotton Bowl. Both teams had one loss, and both were relatively close to Dallas. (Travel was restricted during the war.) The Longhorns, coached by legend Dana X. Bible, were an 8–5 favorite in the contest. Texas had a faster team and deeper reserves. A sellout crowd was expected, and the contest was being broadcast overseas by Mutual for American armed forces.

Although 32,000 tickets were purchased, only 15,000 people showed up due to a downpour. Despite the muddy field, Randolph's quarterback Dobbs had a great day, but he only managed to reach pay dirt once. The game ended in a 7–7 tie, the first tie in Cotton Bowl history.

Both teams received championship watches. Texas coach Bible let the Randolph players take the championship trophy home.

In 2007 the fitness center at Randolph was dedicated to the Ramblers. Walt Parker, the last surviving member of the team, was there for the dedication.

7 One incredible round of golf

When fans speak of great rounds of golf, few people remember Mike Souchak and his score of 257 for 72 holes of golf in 1955—a record that stood for over forty-six years.

The 1955 Texas Open was the oldest tournament on the tour's winter circuit and was played at Brackenridge Golf Course. At that time, many of the tournaments were played on municipal courses. On Thursday, February 17, twenty-seven-year-old Mike Souchak, an ex-Duke football star, shot an incredible 60 on the first day. The final nine holes, Souchak shot a 27 (2, 4, 4, 3, 3, 3, 3, 3, 2), a record that stood until 1970.

Souchak recorded an impressive 68 on Friday, but Saturday's rain caused the condition of the course to deteriorate. Souchak three-putted on the thirteenth hole and lost the lead for a short time. By the end of the day, he was back on top with a round of 64. Despite three great rounds, he had only a three-stroke lead.

The final day drew record crowds to Brackenridge despite near-freezing temperatures. On the eighteenth hole, the jam-packed gallery watched Souchak finish with a 65 for the day and a record 257 for the four-day event. After picking up his ball, he yelled to the crowd, "It's been the greatest thrill I've ever had." For his efforts, he picked up a winner's check of $2,200. The 1955 Texas Open was his first tour victory. In 2001 Mark Calcavecchia finally broke Souchak's record round with a 256 at the Phoenix Open.

Ten San Antonio Sport Franchises and Their Defunct Leagues

1 San Antonio Gunslingers / United States Football League

The Gunslingers were probably the worst-run franchise in this early '80s summer football league. While the New Jersey

Generals played in the luxurious Meadowlands with the backing of Donald Trump and had players like Doug Flutie, Brian Sipe, and Herschel Walker, the Gunslingers played in half-empty Alamo Stadium. The franchise was the embarrassment of the much-maligned league. The team's offices were in a mobile building in Alamo Stadium's parking lot. During a nationally televised contest on ESPN, the power went out at Alamo Stadium. There were even reports that Trump didn't want his team to play the Gunslingers.

Owner Clinton Manges did not help the image of the franchise. Players often went unpaid, and to this day, some of them *still* haven't received payment. The lucky ones who landed paychecks remember racing to the bank to cash them before the team's account was emptied. Manges also promised the league that he would expand Alamo Stadium (primarily used to host high school games) to hold 60,000 in time for the 1986 season, but the only improvements were Astroturf and a fresh coat of paint in the Gunslingers' colors of green and blue. A controversial thirty-year lease, with two ten-year options, was signed, but the team folded, along with the league, after the 1985 season. By suing the National Football League on antitrust grounds, the USFL tried to save itself. It won the case but was awarded only three dollars, after which it closed its turnstiles for good.

2 San Antonio Riders / World League of American Football

The World League of American Football was a spring league established in the early 1990s, featuring teams from the United States, Canada, and Europe. The league was backed by the NFL, which hoped to use the teams to develop players and to create an interest in football overseas. Some, however, saw the venture as an effort to keep rival leagues from forming and competing with the NFL. The franchises were awarded to cities that had been courted by other start-up leagues.

The San Antonio franchise, owned by Larry Benson, was dubbed the Riders and had perhaps the worst combination of team colors in the history of professional sports—brown, red, yellow, and orange. In an effort to exploit a Dallas Cowboys connection, the Riders named Tom Landry Sr. and Tom Landry Jr. as their general managers. The team played their 1991 season in Alamo Stadium and moved to nearby San Marcos for the 1992 season. After the second season, the league suspended play for two years and returned in 1995—minus their American teams. Eventually the league was redubbed the NFL Europe, making the World League of American Football a distant memory.

3 San Antonio Wings / World Football League

This ambitious summer league lasted only two seasons: 1974 and 1975. The Wings played in the final season and posted a 7–4–4 record, leading the Western Division, and a 0–2 record during the fall playoffs. The Wings possessed the league's leading passer, John Walton, who went on to play for the Philadelphia Eagles. In only two years, it lost $30 million and folded on October 2, 1975.

4 Texas Rowels / Major League Rodeo

San Antonio may have never had a major league baseball team, but it was lucky enough to have a Major League Rodeo team. It all started in the spring of 1978. The Western Division included the Denver Stars, the Los Angeles Rough Riders, and the Salt Lake City Buckaroos. The Midwestern Division consisted of the Kansas City Trailblazers, the Tulsa Twisters, and the Texas Rowels, who hailed from San Antonio. (A rowel is the free-wheeling part of the spur.) Major League Rodeo consisted of seven traditional events: team roping, bareback riding, saddle bronc riding, calf roping, steer wrestling, bull riding, and barrel racing, which was an "all cowgirl event." Even after landing a cable television contract, the league failed in the early 1980s.

5 San Antonio Cavaliers / National Bowling League

San Antonio has the distinction of being one of only ten cities to have its own team in the National Bowling League. This ill-fated concept lasted one season. The league had five-man teams bowling head to head in a two-game series. One point was awarded for each win, and a bonus point was awarded for scores over 210. Every ten pins would add another bonus point, and ten bonus points were awarded for a 300 game. Minimum salary for bowlers was $6,000 per season.

The league consisted of the Dallas Broncos, Detroit Thunderbirds, Fort Worth Panthers, Fresno Bombers, Kansas City Stars, Omaha Packers, Los Angeles Toros, Twin Cities Skippers, San Antonio Cavaliers, and New York Gladiators (who were actually from Totowa, N.J.).

The season ran from October 12, 1961, until May 6, 1962. Unfortunately, the era of team bowling was giving way to the advent of the Professional Bowlers Tour. The San Antonio Cavaliers fared little better than the league. With no home lanes, it operated solely as a road club. It folded on December 17, 1961. Only six teams would finish the season. Due to poor attendance and fan disinterest, the league passed into oblivion.

6 San Antonio Thunder / North American Soccer League

This league was formed in 1968 with the merger of the National Professional Soccer League and the United Soccer Association. The San Antonio Thunder were in the league for one year in 1976 before moving to Honolulu and becoming Team Hawaii. The original NASL folded after the 1984 season.

7 San Antonio Spurs / American Basketball Association

The Spurs are still around, but the ABA is long gone. Fondly remembered for its signature red, white, and blue basketball, ABA is the origin of the three-point shot and hosted such greats as Julius Erving, Moses Malone, and George Gervin.

The Dallas Chaparrals never found success in big D, but they were a huge hit when they became the San Antonio Spurs and moved to HemisFair Arena. The silver and black played their first game in October 1973 and were runners-up for the ABA title in 1974. After the 1975–1976 season, the Spurs, the Denver Nuggets, the New York Nets (now Brooklyn), and the Indiana Pacers were asked to join the National Basketball Association. The remaining teams—the Kentucky Colonels, Virginia Squires, and Spirit of St. Louis—followed the ABA and the red, white, and blue ball into oblivion.

The Spurs immediately prospered in the NBA, and in 1979, they came within one game of making it to the finals. The roof of HemisFair Arena was raised in 1977 to accommodate an upper deck, which increased seating from 10,100 to over 15,000.

The only franchise in the city's history to actually outlive its league, the Spurs have had a number of great players, including James Silas (#13) and George Gervin (#44), both of whom have had their numbers retired. Gervin is perhaps San Antonio's most colorful basketball player. Known as the Iceman, he always remained cool and was said to have ice water in his veins. But that trademark coolness had not yet developed when he played for the Eastern Michigan University Hurons; the young Gervin punched a player during a post-season game in 1972. He left the university soon after but was later honored by the school when they retired his jersey.

In 1999 the Spurs became the first former ABA team to win the NBA championship by defeating the New York Knicks four games to one. Led by one-time MVP David Robinson and NBA finals MVP Tim Duncan, the Spurs set an NBA record with twelve straight playoff wins. The Spurs commemorated their ABA days by starting the finals with a ceremonial tip-off using a red, white, and blue ball. Officiating the tip-off was hall-of-famer George "The Iceman" Gervin.

As of 2014 the Spurs have won five NBA titles and are the most successful pro franchise in Texas.

8 San Antonio Iguanas / Central Hockey League

San Antonio's first foray into professional hockey, the Iguanas, are still lovingly remembered by fans for their lunch bucket, workman attitude, and their over-the-top promotions. The mantra often repeated when fans discuss the "Iggies" is "7 Goals and 7 Fights."

The team offered cheap beer, cheap tickets, and a lot of off-the-wall marketing schemes, including sending one lucky fan on a round trip to Hawaii and another on a one-way trip to Laredo. The team played in Freeman Coliseum in the Central Hockey League from 1994 to 2002, taking off a few years when the San Antonio Dragons moved from the more prestigious International Hockey League into the market.

In 2014 the Central Hockey League folded, with the remaining teams absorbed by the East Coast Hockey League.

9 San Antonio Dragons / International Hockey League

After seeing the fan reception of the Iguanas, the higher-level International Hockey League attempted to emulate their success by moving their team, the San Antonio Dragons, into Freeman Coliseum in 1996. After two years, the Dragons were sold, and they promptly changed the name back to the Iguanas and rejoined the Central Hockey League.

In 2001 the International Hockey League shut down after fifty-six years of being one of hockey's top minor leagues, citing competition from the NHL's expansion.

10 San Antonio Texans / Canadian Football League, South Division

Though the Canadian Football League is still around, the South Division, consisting of American teams (south of the Canadian border), existed only from 1993 to 1995.

After the 1994 season, the Sacramento Gold Miners moved to the Alamodome and changed their name to the Texans. The team made it to the South Division Finals in their one and only season, losing to the Baltimore Stallions, who went on to win the Grey Cup before the CFL shut down the South Division for good.

Eight Unusual San Antonio Historic Institutions

1 **Samuel Gompers statue**

Probably the most disliked statue in the city, the Gompers monument rests on Market Street across from the convention center. When the Fairmount Hotel was moving to its new location in 1985, onlookers were rooting for the building to run into the statue.

Gompers established the American Federation of Labor in 1886, which started with 150,000 highly skilled craftsmen, who were not easily replaced by strikebreakers. Therefore, the union was extremely successful in gaining concessions from employers. The labor movement was mainly on the East Coast and had little effect on San Antonio, which was beyond the reach of the Industrial Revolution and early labor activity at the time.

The only reason the statue of Gompers sits downtown is that he died in San Antonio, at the St. Anthony Hotel in 1924. He was returning from an international labor conference in Mexico, and his train stopped overnight here. AFL-CIO gave the monument to the city in 1974.

2 **North Pole marker**

Ever wonder how many miles it is to the North Pole? Someone obviously did. At the southeast corner of Dewey Street and

The Samuel Gompers statue on Market Street, across from the Convention Center.

Main Avenue, behind San Antonio College, sits a marker that points out that the North Pole is 4,189 miles away. For many years, the origin of the sign was a great mystery.

The building, which has passed through many hands, was once home to the Evergreen Drugstore. The store was owned by R. T. and Victor Jones from 1920 to 1943. R. T. Jones's daughter-in-law is Marianna Jones, who later became president of the San Antonio Conservation Society. In the March 1995 issue of the *S.A.C.S. News* she recounted the story of the sign:

> About 1940, in the midst of one of the coldest winters in San Antonio history, a car struck and damaged the Main Avenue storefront. As so often happens, the tile could not be matched and, while the Jones brothers pondered solutions, a customer complained about the incredible weather, saying it must be as bad as that at the North Pole. A discussion about how far it must be to the North Pole ensued, so "RT" vowed to write Rand McNally to find out—and in due time an answer arrived: "4189 miles." Coincidentally, a cement worker involved in another project in the area, hearing of the Jones brothers difficulties with their storefront damage, offered to create a sign in the problem place. RT, quite a prankster, thought the North Pole idea would be a great joke, hence the relatively well known sign.

3 Pat Memorial

Located on Wilson Avenue in Fort Sam Houston, this memorial was erected in honor of Pat the Horse, who retired after twenty-six years of military service when the 12th Field Artillery Unit was motorized. Pat died in 1953, at the age of forty-five, but his memory lives on.

4 Water Museum

Established in 1976 in the historic Schroeder-Yturri home on the City Water Board property on Commerce Street, the

Water Museum was run by the water board but had irregular hours and was such a well-kept secret that even many water board employees knew nothing of it. A brass plaque outside the building proudly proclaims the museum's existence, despite the fact that the exhibits were moved to the basement when the board needed more office space, effectively closing the obscure attraction.

5 Shrine of Our Lady of Czestochowa

Located at 138 Beethoven Street on the east side, this shrine commemorates a thousand years of Polish Christianity. Built in 1966, it honors the black Madonna, Poland's most important religious icon. In addition, the pink granite memorial also honors silent film star Pola Negri, who made San Antonio her home in the twilight of her life. It is the only shrine anywhere that honors both. Nuns from Poland staff the facility, and masses in Polish are held there daily.

6 Ursuline Academy's curious clock tower

When the old convent and school were built on Convent Street, it was on the edge of town. Since no one lived to the north of the academy, the tower was built without a clock facing that direction. The young ladies who attended the academy used to say that there was no clock on the north side because they would not be caught giving the time of day to a Yankee.

7 Old Spanish Trail marker

In 1929 Bexar County had the most paved roads in America, including the very first one to cross the nation, the Old Spanish Trail. Probably the most used road, the Old Spanish Trail is often confused with the Camino Real, established by the Spanish, which is believed to be the oldest road in America. The Old Spanish Trail was actually started in 1915 and completed in 1924, making San Antonio the geographic center of modern paved thoroughfare. Today, Interstate 10 follows the route set by that early road. Sadly, there are few reminders of the once great road. Behind an electrical box on the corner of Fredericksburg and Vance Jackson Roads is a stone bench bearing the wrought iron letters "OST," one of the last relics of the Old Spanish Trail.

8 Barney Smith's Toilet Seat Art Museum

Located at 239 Abiso Avenue in Alamo Heights, Barney Smith has over 500 decorated toilet seats that hang for public viewing. Smith originally decorated the seats as a hobby, but a local artist visiting his yard sale noticed the unusual art form and alerted a local TV station. After the station ran a story on the objets d'art, Smith was overwhelmed with attention. In August 1992 he opened his garage as a museum. When visiting, be sure to see the toilet seat that features a chunk of the Berlin Wall, the one with barbed wire from Auschwitz, and the one with a piece of the space shuttle Challenger. Over a thousand people a year now visit the retiree's attraction. Barney asks that you call first before stopping by.

Eleven Favorite San Antonio Ghost Stories

Every town has tales of spirits that inhabit the area, and San Antonio is no exception. What follows are some of the city's most popular.

1 The ghost crossing

Perhaps the most popular tale, the ghost crossing has enticed thousands of San Antonians to trek out to an obscure southeast railroad crossing to participate in an eerie phenomenon. The ghost crossing is on Shane Road, where it intersects with the Southern Pacific rail line. According to the legend, a school bus full of kids stalled on the tracks and was hit by a train. Today if a motorist stops before the tracks and places the car in neutral, the ghosts of those children will push the vehicle over the tracks.

To visit the crossing, take Presa south off SE Military Drive. Turn right on Southton Road, then right again on Shane. Turn off your engine and give it a try. If you're brave, visit the crossing at night. You will be amazed when your car mysteriously moves across the tracks. Is it an optical illusion? Are you really moving downhill? Or is your car being pushed across by ghosts?

Part of this ghostly tale is that the nearby subdivision has streets named for the children who perished in the supposed accident. Actually they are simply the names of the neighborhood developer's grandchildren.

2 The ghostly nuns

The basement of Santa Rosa Hospital is said to be the haunting grounds for these spectral beings. The ghosts are believed to be the spirits of five nuns who died on October 30, 1912, after trying to rescue children from a burning orphanage. The wooden building of the St. John's Orphan Asylum, which went up in flames that night, was located across from the hospital at the corner of Houston and San Saba Streets.

3 The Menger ghost

Said to haunt the old portion of the Menger Hotel, Sallie White was a hotel chambermaid who was murdered by her husband. This poltergeist is rather stubborn, appearing only when she pleases.

4 The Alamo ghosts

Many guests who have stayed at the Menger Hotel in rooms that overlook the Alamo have said that they have spotted the ghosts of the Alamo defenders. Legend states that General Andrade of the Mexican army planned to destroy the Alamo after the Battle of San Jacinto. But when he ordered his troops to do so, the ghosts of Travis, Bowie, and the others appeared with flaming swords, screaming, "Do not touch these walls!"

On Nacogdoches near Loop 1604 sits a stone tower atop a hill. It is said that this tower is also haunted by ghosts from the Alamo days. Lights are often seen at the tower at night, and many believe that the tower was a lookout post for the Alamo and that the lights belong to the spirits of the sentry.

5 The dancing diablo

The site for this terrible tale is the El Camaroncito Nite Club, located at 411 W. Old Highway 90. It's said that in the 1970s a debonair patron was dancing with many different women one evening, and at some point, one lady looked down and noticed that the dapper dancer had the feet of a chicken. This is of course the sign of the devil, so the woman screamed, and El Diablo ran from the club. El Camaroncito Nite Club is now closed, but the chicken-footed dancer has been reported at other establishments throughout the years.

6 The ghosts of Milam Square

Few people realize that the public park between Santa Rosa Hospital and El Mercado was once a cemetery for the Canary Islanders. It is said that if you pass through the square with evil thoughts, you will be visited by spirits.

7 The Converse wolfman

Set many years ago in the area of Skull Creek near FM 1518, the legend tells of a thirteen-year-old boy, who spent most of his time reading. The father thought the boy was too much of a bookworm, so he bought him a rifle, thinking that by forcing the child to go hunting, he could reform him. After his first day out with the gun, the boy came home and told his parents of a wolfman-type creature in the woods. The father, not believing the boy, told him to go out and not to return until he had killed something. When the young hunter did not come home, a search party was organized. At the creek, the boy was found dead, and the wolfman was feasting on his body. The wolfman supposedly returns to the creek during full moons, and when he does, the water in the creek turns blood red.

8 The donkey lady

Also called La Llorona, the donkey lady was a beautiful poor girl who fell in love with a rich aristocrat. Because they were of different classes, they were forbidden to marry. The young lady thus became the man's mistress and bore him several children. Some versions say she drowned the children because she was poor and could not afford to keep them. Others say she drowned them because she was evil. Regardless, because of her awful actions, she was condemned for eternity to be a ghost with a donkey's head on her beautiful body.

La Llorona has been reported on Applewhite Road near Zarzamora and at the intersection of Blanco and Lockhill-Selma. She also has been spotted by teenagers who go to Espada Park to neck. The legend is often told by superstitious parents to warn their children of the ghost that haunts youngsters who play near forbidden waters.

9 The Navarro House ghost

This downtown landmark is the former home of José Antonio Navarro, signer of the Texas Declaration of Independence. Believers in the paranormal have heard footsteps and spotted furniture that has been moved under mysterious circumstances. Some say the ghost is the home's namesake; others say it is a slain prostitute, a murdered bartender, or a Confederate deserter.

10 The seven-foot Chinese woman

This large Asian ghost haunts an old cemetery near Stinson Field. One version of the tale claims the seven-foot-tall local woman killed herself because her Chinese contemporaries ridiculed her for being so tall. Some say she died in a fire. The same area is said to be haunted by a bearded lady as well.

11 Midget mansion
This legend was fueled by the overactive imaginations of teenagers who attended Marshall and Clark high schools. For years, students went after dark to an old abandoned home situated between Datapoint Drive and Medical Drive near the Medical Center to tell the story of a mansion run by evil midgets.

Eleven Facts the Author Felt Belonged in the Book

1 San Antonio is one of the few cities in the country that has a European-style youth hostel. It is located next to the Camp Bullis Guest House at the corner of Grayson and Pierce.

2 San Antonio has the only branch of the National Autonomous University of Mexico located outside Mexico. The school is located at HemisFair Park.

3 San Antonio is home to Texas's first Maronite church, an Eastern Rite of the Catholic Church that has 700,000 members in Lebanon, Syria, Cyprus, and Jordan, as well as 300,000 in the United States. St. George Maronite was formed in San Antonio in 1925. The original church on the city's west side was lost to freeway construction, and in 1980, a new church was built on the north side for $1 million.

4 Henry Thomas, the young star of the blockbuster movie *E. T.,* is from San Antonio. Thomas was a student in the East

Central school district when he made the film, and he later attended East Central High School.

5   Woodlawn Lake, originally known as West End Lake, was part of West End Town, the city's first suburb. The area was connected to downtown via a trolley line. A levy was built over Alazán Creek for the track, and the dirt came from what is now the casting pond. The lake became known as Woodlawn Lake in the 1920s.

6   Michael Nesmith of the Monkees was a student at San Antonio College. His mother also made her mark on the world, inventing Liquid Paper.

7   Carol Burnett was born in San Antonio. She lived at 2803 W. Commerce and attended Crockett Elementary School before moving west.

8   In the early part of the twentieth century, San Antonio was home to a burgeoning film industry, drawn to the city by its warm weather and variety of terrain. Moviemakers shot dozens of films here. The most successful company was Star Films located in the old Hot Wells Hotel.

9   The city hosted a European aerialist troupe during its annual Fiesta celebration in the 1950s. The European troupe performed twice daily on a high wire suspended over Houston Street. These aerialists and other performers walked and rode bicycles high above Alamo Plaza without a net.

10   Shaquille O'Neal is a graduate of Cole High School in San Antonio, where he helped win the state basketball championship

11   When I was in college, a friend told me the Butter Krust Bakery on Broadway had a door in the back where they would sell loaves of fresh bread off the assembly line for a dollar. Watching the loaves crawl along the conveyor belt through the windows on Broadway, I was intrigued. One day we walked through the bakery's back door, and an employee asked if she could help us. We said we wanted to get a loaf of hot bread. She looked at us and asked simply, "Sliced or unsliced?"

Twelve San Antonio Outings

You've visited the Alamo, the missions, and the zoo. You've read this entire book, and you still cannot find anything to do. Why not try one of these outings?

1   Walk the Texas Star Trail.
The San Antonio Conservation Society and the Texas Sesquicentennial Committee have created a unique walking tour of downtown. Guides to the tour can be acquired at the Conservation Society headquarters or at the Visitors Bureau on Alamo Plaza. Markers inserted in the sidewalk throughout downtown make the trail easy to follow.

2   Visit the city's massive east side cemetery complex.
Take New Braunfels Avenue to Commerce Street and discover blocks of grave sites that include many of the founders of San Antonio. These grave sites date back to a time when this area was on the outskirts of the city on a hill overlooking downtown. Names such as Kampmann, Menger, Steves, and Groos can be found throughout the area. An old Confederate cemetery is hidden off Commerce Street. Texas's only Confederate general is buried there, as are 206 veterans of the Civil War, including soldiers from Germany, Scotland, France, and England who fought for the South.

Many of the city's early churches had plots in this complex. St. Joseph's Cemetery is filled with many of the German elite of early San Antonio. Clara Driscoll, savior of the Alamo, is buried in a tomb on the west edge of the Alamo Masonic Cemetery, just off Commerce. Sidney Brooks (for whom Brooks Air Force Base is named) is buried a few yards from there. Socialite Sandra West is buried in her Ferrari somewhere amid the graves.

San Antonio's first national cemetery is located here. It is the final resting place of Harry Wurzbach, Lieutenant George Kelly, John L. Bullis, and a host of other familiar names. Fortunately, this is one of the few parts of the complex that is in decent shape. Many of the other plots are overgrown with weeds and have had tombstones destroyed. In the last few years, public awareness of the cemeteries has grown, and plans are being discussed to improve the facilities.

3 Dine at a converted gas station or icehouse.

San Antonio may have set a record for the number of gas stations that have been converted into dining establishments. The most prominent may be Chris Madrid's on Blanco, or try Deco Pizzeria on Fredericksburg Road.

4 Discover the city's public murals.

Start at the post office on Alamo Plaza. In the lobby is an excellent example of the WPA era's "art for the millions." The mural, painted by Howard N. Cook, depicts Texas history from the time of Indians to its industrialization. The sixteen panels make the piece the nation's largest true fresco mural.

The exterior of Santa Rosa Children's Hospital features a ninety-foot mural dubbed *The Spirit of Healing*. Created by Jesse Treviño, the piece has over 150,000 pieces of cut ceramic tile and took three years to create. Alamo Stadium features a mural of area sports above the main entrance. Inside the main concourse to the Lila Cockrell Theatre at the Convention Center are two pieces that renowned artist

You Are Not Forgotten mural on West Commerce and Colorado Streets.

Lideres de la communidad mural on Colorado and Buena Vista Streets.

Juan O'Gorman created for HemisFair '68 reflecting the fair's theme, "A Confluence of Civilizations."

Check out Terry Ybañez's striking tribute to Emma Tenayuca on S. Presa in Southtown. And finally, visit Trinity University's Coates Library, home to the world's largest montage mural. *Man's Evolving Images: Printing and Writing*, by James Sicner, wraps around the staircase and is eighty feet long and fifteen feet high.

5   Attend a Catholic mass.

Downtown San Antonio features four Catholic churches, all with remarkable features. Other notable churches include the Shrine of the Little Flower and the Chapel at Our Lady of the Lake University. Many of the area churches regularly feature mariachi masses and services in a variety of languages including Polish and Italian. The city's most famous service is arguably the Mission San José's Mariachi Mass. Attending a mass in a historic mission is a true San Antonio experience. All of the historic sites are home to active parishes.

6   Visit the Blue Star Arts Complex.

The converted warehouse compound across from the Pioneer Flour Mill features artist studios, shops, galleries, artist living spaces, performance places, and a brew pub. The first Friday of every month, the complex opens its doors for a night of food, music, and gallery openings.

7   Stroll through San Antonio's Deco district.

This inner loop section of Fredericksburg Road was one part of the Old Spanish Trail. It has the city's finest collection of Art Deco architecture. The neighborhood was in decline until the '80s, when community leaders banded together to save the area. Finish off your visit with a stop at the Tip Top Cafe. Open since 1938, it's famous for its onion rings and chicken-fried steak.

8 **Visit a homestead that dates back to the Alamo.**
Phil Hardberger Park on the north side was acquired by the city in 2007 and sits on what was the last whole parcel of farmland in the city limits. The dairy barn and the old stone home date back to the 1870s. Fighting off development and the Wurzbach Parkway, the Voelcker family remained on the land until Max and Minnie Voelcker died in 1980 and 2000, respectively. Their homestead was restored and is now part of the park, whose paths lead to Salado Creek Greenway, one of the city's most extensive trail systems.

9 **Attend one of San Antonio's festivals.**
Perhaps no city has as many festivals as San Antonio. We love them. The biggest, of course, is Fiesta, closely followed by the Folklife Festival. Other popular ones include the Tejano-Conjunto Festival, the Lowrider Festival, and Wurstfest in nearby New Braunfels. The San Antonio Stock Show and Rodeo, while not technically a festival, takes up two weeks in the city's busy social schedule.

10 **Check out 20 million bats.**
Bracken Bat Cave just outside the city limits has the largest collection of Mexican Free Tail bats in the world, estimated at 20 million during the summer months. The cave and the surrounding acreage are owned by Bat Conservation International, which offers occasional opportunities for the public to view the cave up close.

11 **Visit the city's museums.**
In 2015 the San Antonio Children's Museum moved from downtown to Broadway and was redubbed the Do-Seum. Designed by Lake/Flato architects, the museum—along with the expanding Witte Museum, the Botanical Gardens, and the Pearl complex—has made Broadway one of the most exciting avenues in San Antonio.

12 Enjoy some of San Antonio's unique culinary treasures.

Start off at Schilo's Deli on Commerce Street and try the homemade root beer and Mama Schilo's split pea soup. This German restaurant has remained virtually unchanged in the last fifty years. Then try the sopa Azteca, served only on Saturdays, at El Mirador in Southtown. Finally, travel to Alamo Plaza and finish with a bowl of mango ice cream from the Colonial Room in the Menger Hotel.

NAMES

San Antonio. The river (and subsequently the city) was named for St. Anthony de Padua, because the river was discovered on his feast day, June 13, 1691, by Spanish explorers. Domingo Terán del los Ríos, governor of the New Philippines (as Texas was called then), and Padre Damián Massanet, senior chaplain, were both with the expedition party that discovered the river, and both claim responsibility in their journals for the name.

Bexar County. On May 5, 1718, Spanish governor Martín de Alarcón proclaimed the establishment on the river the Royal Presidio of San Antonio de Bexar, named in honor of the family of the dukes of Bexar.

Castroville. This small South Texas town is named after Henri Castro, who was born in France of Portuguese Jewish parents. Castro served on Napoleon's Guard of Honor, fought to defend Paris in 1814, and was an officer in the Legion of Honor in 1818. While in Texas in 1842, Castro entered into a contract with the Texan government to settle a colony of French immigrants. The town was founded in 1844, mainly by families from the province of Alsace in France.

Mission San Antonio de Valero. The Alamo as it was originally known was named by Father Antonio de San Buenaventura y Olivares in honor of the viceroy, Marqués de Valero.

The Alamo. In 1803 Mission San Antonio de Valero became secularized and was later a military outpost. The first military reinforcements to arrive, composed of a hundred lancers, were the Alamo Company, named for their hometown, Alamo de Parras in Coahuila, Mexico. The mission became known as the Pueblo de la Compañía del Alamo, which was later shortened to simply the Alamo.

San Pedro Springs. Named by Father Isidro Félix de Espinosa on April 13, 1709, when the expedition discovered the springs. The springs are named for St. Peter, or San Pedro.

Medina River. The river was crossed in 1869 by explorer Alonso de León, who named it for Spanish scholar and engineer Pedro Medina. The Medina River was once recognized as the western boundary of Texas.

Henry B. González Convention Center. This massive downtown complex is named in honor of longtime San Antonio congressman Henry B. González. González, a former San Antonio city councilman and the first Hispanic member of Congress, is best known for his long speeches on a variety of topics and for punching out a man twenty years his junior at Earl Abel's Restaurant after being called a communist.

Lila Cockrell Theatre. Named after the city's first woman mayor. The two-term mayor also has an apartment complex for the elderly named after her.

Arneson River Theatre. Named after E. P. Arneson, the first consulting engineer on the River Walk, who died in 1938, before construction got under way.

Callaghan Road. Named after former San Antonio mayor Alfred Callaghan, who was elected to office in 1947. Both his father and grandfather were also San Antonio mayors.

Eisenhauer Road. It's named not after the former president, but for Otto Eisenhauer, the son of a German immigrant who farmed on the northeast side for nearly seventy years.

Jones-Maltsberger Road. This road once led to two dairies, one owned by the Jones family and the other owned by the Maltsberger family. Rittiman Road and Walzem Road are also named for family-owned dairies.

Perrin-Beitel Road. This road led to land owned by the Perrins and the Beitels. Near the main post office on Perrin-Beitel is an old cemetery for the two families. West Avenue, De Zavala,

Evers, Eckert, Babcock, Huebner, and Marbach are all named for the people who built the roads out to their land.

McCullough Avenue. Named after Rev. John McCullough of First Presbyterian Church in San Antonio in 1846. People from the north side took this road to reach the downtown church.

Belknap Street. Named after Augustus Belknap, who put in the city's first streetcars, which were mule-driven down San Pedro Avenue.

Brees Boulevard. Named for Lieutenant General Herbert J. Brees, who commanded the Third U.S. Army headquartered in the Smith-Young Tower (now the Tower Life Building). Brees was stationed in San Antonio from October 1940 to May 1941.

Flores Street. One of the oldest streets in San Antonio, this thoroughfare was named in honor of Nicolas Flores y Valdés, who fought against Indian raids during the Aguayo Expedition in 1721. The expedition fought to open supply routes to the area's missions. Some sources say this street was named Flores Street (meaning "flowers" in Spanish) simply because of the many flowers that grew along the boulevard.

Travis, Crockett, Bowie, Bonham, and Milam Streets. All were named after the heroes of the Alamo and the Texas Revolution.

St. Mary's Street. Named in honor of the Brothers of St. Mary's, who came to San Antonio in 1851 to start St. Mary's University.

Main Avenue. Originally Acequia Street, the name was changed to Main Avenue because it was often referred to as Main Street since Main High School was located there.

College Street. This downtown street was so named because it ran by St. Mary's University. The school has since moved to the northwest side of town, and La Mansión del Rio hotel now occupies the site.

Soledad Street. At one time, this street had only one house on it, so it was named *Soledad*, Spanish for "lonely."

Convent Street. Named for the Ursuline nuns, whose convent was located on the street. The building is now home to the Southwest School of Art.

Dolorosa Street. *Dolorosa* is Spanish, meaning "sadness." Some sources say the street was named for the Virgin Mary, mother of sadness. Others say it was named the street of sadness because it led to Mexico, and many wives saw their soldier husbands leave town on the road, never to return. Still others say the name refers to mourners who witnessed a mass execution on Military Plaza in the early 1800s.

Kenmore Street. This small street once separated Sears from its parking garage and is named for the store's line of appliances.

Jack White Street. This small street between Nueva and Villita Streets was originally built by the Plaza Hotel (now Grenada Homes) as a place for cabs to park and for motorists to turn around. The street was unnamed for many years and caused a problem for the hotel's proprietor, who had trouble giving directions to the business located on the end of the nameless avenue. The hotel operator was named, you guessed it, Jack White. One of the first proponents of the River Walk, White later became mayor of San Antonio, thereby acquiring the influence to have the street named after himself.

Broadway. This avenue originally had three names: Avenue C, Lasoya, and River Avenue. The street received the name Broadway at the suggestion of Alamo Heights residents, who thought the street that led to their enclave should have an exceptional name.

Navarro Street. Named after José Antonio Navarro, one of the signers of the Texas Declaration of Independence.

Nogalitos Street. Spanish, meaning "little pecan trees," which used to line this street.

Zarzamora Street. Spanish, meaning "thorny mulberries." The Spanish who settled San Antonio discovered dewberries on the site. Not knowing what they were, they assumed they were some sort of thorny mulberry and named the street after them.

Presa Street. This street once led to the Espada dam, and *presa* is Spanish for "dam."

King's Highway. This picturesque avenue near the city's north side is anything but a highway. It was named after the ancient El Camino Real (Spanish for "King's Highway"), a road built to connect the missions of Texas. Designating the course of the road are 123 markers throughout Texas. One marker rests in San Pedro Park and was dedicated on March 2, 1920.

Charles Anderson Loop (aka Loop 1604). The city's outer loop bears the name of a former Bexar County judge. The honorable Charles W. Anderson served twenty-five years on the bench, despite having to walk on crutches after losing part of his foot in World War II. Anderson died of cancer in 1964.

Josephine Tobin Drive. An expansive sign marks this small stretch of road that snakes around Woodlawn Lake and is named after the only woman who was both a mother and a daughter of San Antonio mayors. Her father was Mayor John William Smith, and her son was Mayor John Tobin.

Harry Wurzbach Road. Named after four-term U.S. Congressman Harry M. Wurzbach, who served in the House from 1921 to 1932. Wurzbach was also a corporal in the 1st Texas Volunteer Infantry, a four-term county judge, and a county attorney. Wurzbach drew his support from the area's large German population, which made him a virtual shoo-in for Congress. Born on May 19, 1874, he was the first Republican from Texas to be elected for more than two terms to the House. He died November 6, 1931, and is buried in the forgotten U.S. Cemetery on the city's east side.

Michael Nesmith Street. This avenue in a subdivision in Leon Valley is named after the former Monkees rock group member. Nesmith lived in San Antonio for a time and attended San Antonio College. The street was named by Nesmith's uncle, who was one of the developers of Leon Valley.

General McMullen Drive. Named for a former commander of Kelly Air Force Base.

Cupples Road. This road is named after Colonel George Cupples, a former agent of Henri Castro.

Basse Road. Named for Edgar A. Basse Sr., founder of the Piggly Wiggly supermarket chain.

Pat Booker Road. This road, which leads from I-35 to Randolph Air Force Base, is named for Captain Francis "Pat" Booker, who died in a plane crash. Captain Booker served under William M. Randolph in an army air squadron in the Canal Zone.

Bandera Road. Many roads were named for their destination. Bandera Road led to Bandera, Blanco Road led to Blanco, Fredericksburg Road led to Fredericksburg, and it's obvious where Austin Highway led to. When the interstate highway system was completed, many of the roads were incorporated into the highway, and they no longer go all the way to their respective towns. Other roads named after the towns they led to include New Braunfels, Nacogdoches, Pleasanton, Wetmore, Corpus Christi, and Somerset.

Stinson Field. The small municipal airport located on the city's south side is named for the Stinson family, who operated a flying school there in the 1910s. The airport is one of the three oldest in the country. The airport was renamed Winburn Field after a plane crash on October 15, 1927, took the life of *San Antonio Express* reporter Bill Winburn. On July 15, 1936, the field was renamed Stinson Field. During World War II, Stinson Field was taken over by the Army Air Corps for pilot training. Interestingly enough, Marjorie Stinson trained World War I pilots on the same field that had been the site of her private flying school almost thirty years earlier.

Kelly Field. This former air force base was named for Army Lieutenant George E. M. Kelly, who died in a plane crash at Fort Sam Houston on May 10, 1911. Kelly was the first military pilot to lose his life in a plane accident. Because of his death, all military flights were halted for three years. Kelly is buried in San Antonio in the first military cemetery, located in the city's east side cemetery complex. Kelly received his commission and his wings posthumously.

Brooks AFB. Named for Cadet Sidney Johnson Brooks Jr., the first San Antonio native to lose his life in a World War I–related activity. Brooks died on November 13, 1917, after apparently fainting during a training flight from Hondo Air Field to Kelly Field. Brooks is buried in San Antonio but not in the U.S. Cemetery. To find his grave site, look for the western edge of the city's east side cemetery complex, off Commerce Street. The Brooks family plots are located across from Clara Driscoll's tomb.

Randolph AFB. Named for Captain William M. Randolph, who was killed in a plane crash at Kelly Field (some reports say Gorman Field) in 1928. Randolph was on the committee that helped design the base.

Lackland AFB. Named for General Frank D. Lackland, who was the pioneer commander of Kelly Field. The area now occupied by Lackland AFB was originally a bombing range for Kelly. After Pearl Harbor, it became the San Antonio Aviation Cadet Center. In 1947 it became Lackland AFB.

Wilford Hall Ambulatory Surgical Center. Named in 1963 for Major General Wilford Hall, who was stationed at Randolph Field in the 1930s. Dr. Hall was a pioneer in the field of aviation surgery.

Fort Sam Houston. Named after the general who led Texas troops to victory over Santa Anna in the Battle of San Jacinto. The military hero, and soon-to-be Texas governor, defeated Santa Anna in eighteen minutes.

Brooke Army Medical Center. Originally Brooke General Hospital, it was named in honor of Brigadier General Roger Brooke, the former commanding officer at the old post hospital. The original hospital opened in 1938 at a cost of $2 million and was later redeveloped. The new BAMC at Fort Sam Houston is home to the military's finest burn facility and the U.S. Army's medical school.

Funston Loop. This Fort Sam street, with some of the most picturesque homes in the city (not to mention some of the most beautiful military quarters ever), is named after General Frederick Funston, commander of the post from 1915 until his death in 1917.

Camp Bullis. Named for General John Lapham Bullis, who in 1873 took command of a company of Seminole Indian Scouts and defended settlers from hostile Indians. Bullis died on May 26, 1911, and is buried in the U.S. Cemetery on the city's east side.

Audie Murphy Memorial Veterans Hospital. There was a time when every American knew the exploits of Audie Murphy, a young Texas boy who became the most decorated soldier of World War II, with twelve medals of valor, including the Distinguished Service Cross and the Congressional Medal of Honor, the nation's two highest awards. The story of a young soldier from Greenville, Texas, who had killed 240 Germans ended up in *Life* magazine, and Audie Murphy became a national icon. After the war, Murphy headed to Hollywood, where he starred in mostly westerns and war movies (including his autobiography). He died in a plane crash in 1971.

Judge John H. Wood Courthouse. This circular building on Hemisfair Plaza was originally the U.S. Pavilion for the World's Fair. After the event, it became a courthouse. It was eventually renamed for Judge John Wood, who was killed in June 1979 by a single bullet, while leaving his San Antonio home for work one morning. He was the first federal judge murdered in more than a century. Known as "Maximum John" because of his strict punishments, the judge was feared by many involved in drug trafficking. At the time of the murder, Wood was scheduled to preside over the trial of reputed drug lord Jimmy Chagra. An interesting note: the man convicted of murdering the judge was Charles Harrelson. His trial was held in the Wood Courthouse and presided over by one of Wood's pallbearers. His son is actor Woody Harrelson.

Mayor Maury Maverick Plaza. This open space in La Villita is named in honor of the mayor who organized the restoration of La Villita. A bust of Maverick is on display in front of the plaza on Alamo Street.

O'Neil Ford Plaza. This small, forgotten place behind the Little Church of La Villita is named for the architect of its restoration. Ford was one of the city's most noted architects and was one of the first to be concerned with the conservation of historic structures. Some of his most notable works include Trinity University and the Tower of the Americas.

Rose Window. Mission San José, built in 1720, is known for its beautiful Rose Window. The name of the delicately carved stone window frame is somewhat of a mystery, because there are no roses whatsoever on the piece. Although most people believe that the sculptor was Pedro Huizar and that he crafted the piece for his love, a woman named Rosa, Huizar arrived in Texas after the window was already carved. So the true sculptor is unknown. First-time visitors to Mission San José may recognize the Rose Window because it is said to be the most photographed window in the world.

Main Plaza, or Plaza de las Islas. Spanish for "Plaza of the Islands," this downtown park across from the courthouse was named for the first settlers of San Antonio from the Canary Islands.

Military Plaza. City Hall now sits on Military Plaza, which was once the social center of downtown. Chili queens, merchants, and a variety of characters gathered there throughout the 1800s. It received its name from the previous century, when it had barracks for a garrison on the north side of the plaza. The east side of the plaza was designated for the Catholic Church (San Fernando Cathedral is situated on the east side), the west side was set aside for civil and military officials (the Spanish Governor's Palace sits on the west side), and the south side was reserved for settlers.

Brackenridge Park. Opened in 1900, the park is named for George Brackenridge, one of San Antonio's greatest philanthropists. Brackenridge started one of San Antonio's first banking institutions, financially supported the city's water system, and worked to develop public schools. The land that is now the park was donated by Brackenridge. A statue of the city's patriarch stands at the Broadway entrance to the park.

Milam Park. This downtown plaza, sandwiched between Santa Rosa Hospital and El Mercado, is actually a cemetery named for Ben Milam, who came to Texas in 1818 and was active in the Texas Revolution. He died in 1835, when he was hit by a sniper's bullet. The bridge on the River Walk behind the Petroleum Commerce building has a mural depicting Milam's death. Milam is buried on the west end of the block-long park, while some of the original Canary Islanders are buried on the east side.

Mahncke Park. This small and mostly undeveloped park situated at Broadway and Funston Place provides a pleasant green space amid the hustle of Broadway. The park is named for Ludwig Mahncke, the first park commissioner for the city. Mahncke was instrumental in securing the donation of land for Brackenridge Park.

Lambert Beach. The north end of Brackenridge Park is known as Lambert Beach, named for Ray Lambert, a popular park commissioner from the 1920s who was responsible for the Sunken Gardens. At one time this was a popular swimming spot on the San Antonio River. You can still see the changing rooms next to the zoo fence.

McAllister Park/McAllister Freeway. Named for former mayor and founder of San Antonio Savings, W. W. McAllister. The mayor was instrumental in getting U.S. 281 built as a passageway to the north side.

Phil Hardberger Park. After Max and Minnie Voelcker died, Mayor Hardberger was instrumental in acquiring their dairy for the park in 2007. It had been the last whole parcel of farmland left in the city.

O. P. Schnabel Park. This city park was named after the founder of the Beautify San Antonio Association and the Beautify Texas Council. Though Schnabel died in 1987, the namesake park was established when he was still living.

Koehler Park. This park is adjacent to Brackenridge Park, though few people realize that they are two distinct parks. It was donated to the city in 1915 by Emma Koehler, former president of the Pearl Brewing Company. The Koehler estate (now the Koehler Cultural Center), a block-long residence adjacent to San Antonio College, is now used by the school. Other city parks named after people who donated land to the city because they wanted a park in their neighborhood include Raymond Russell Park (donated by Meta and Raymond Russell in 1951), Pletz Park (donated by Leo Pletz in 1963), and Orsinger Park (donated by Ward and Genevieve Orsinger in 1980).

Koger Stokes Softball Center. This complex located in San
Pedro Park is named after the organizer and former president of
the Texas Amateur Athletic Foundation.

Dignowity Park. Also known as Dignowity Hill, it's named for the
family who built a large home dubbed Harmony House in this
once prominent east side neighborhood. The house was torn
down in 1926, and the land is now a city park. The head of the
family was Czechoslovakian Anthony M. Dignowity, who came
to America in 1832, after participating in a failed Polish revolt
against Russia. He studied medicine in Mississippi before settling in San Antonio. With the approaching Civil War, the young
doctor became quite vocal in his opposition to slavery and
fled to the North when concerns for his safety grew. When he
returned to San Antonio in 1869, he found that his assets had
been seized. He died in 1875, after spending his last six years
trying to recover his property. The east side Dignowity neighborhood received historic designation in 1985. Older than the
King William neighborhood, it was the first fashionable area
outside the city's core. In the nineteenth century, the area was a
haven for the rich who wanted to escape the hustle and bustle of
San Antonio.

King William district. This historic neighborhood south of
downtown was once the bastion of wealthy Germans who settled in San Antonio in the nineteenth century. The area became
known as the King Wilhelm neighborhood after King Wilhelm I
of Prussia, who later became a German emperor.

St. Peter Claver Church and the Healy-Murphy Center.
This Catholic church on San Antonio's east side is named for
a Jesuit missionary who worked in South America with African
slaves. Peter Claver was canonized in 1888, and the chapel built
that same year was the first church in the country to be named
for him. The parish was under the supervision of the Josephite
Fathers until 1964, when it became affiliated with St. Joseph's. It
was the first Catholic church for African Americans in this part
of Texas. St. Peter Claver Academy, adjacent to the church, is
now home to Healy-Murphy Learning Center and Child Care

Center. Margaret Murphy, a widow of a former Corpus Christi mayor, founded the academy. She devoted her time and money to serving poor African Americans after hearing a sermon denouncing the practice of having nonwhites sit at the back of the church.

Little Flower Church. This Catholic church was named for Sister Thérèse, a Carmelite nun, who was known as the Little Flower. Also called the Shrine of the Little Flower, the church's official name is the Parish of Our Lady of Mount Carmel and St. Thérèse.

Joe and Harry Freeman Coliseum. The facility was originally named the Bexar County Coliseum and opened October 19, 1949. Then it was called the Joe Freeman Coliseum, after the stock show and rodeo founder, who died in 1975. The name was later changed to include Joe's brother Harry, a lifelong stock show board member, who died in 1985.

Blossom Athletic Center. This complex, which consists of various athletic facilities for the North East Independent School District, is named in honor of Virgil T. Blossom, a former superintendent, who died in 1965. Blossom was instrumental in initiating growth in the fledgling district but is better known for his school integration plan in Little Rock, Arkansas. The plan was opposed by the Arkansas governor, who sent National Guardsmen to block integration at Central High School. But President Eisenhower used federal troops to enforce Blossom's plan.

Paul Taylor Field House. This Northside Independent School District gymnasium is named after a popular Northside coach who died of cancer.

Leal Middle School. This south side school is named after Armando Leal, who graduated from Harlandale High School in 1964 and died in Vietnam in 1967, while trying to save wounded marines.

Churchill High School. This high school is named after the British chief of state because a former school board member had a particular fondness for Churchill. The North East

Independent School District has a policy of naming their high schools after famous Americans, but Churchill slipped by because trustee Maxwell Higginbotham argued that since Churchill's mother was American, so was he.

Gus Garcia Junior High. Garcia was the first Mexican American elected to the San Antonio Independent School District's board of trustees, but he gained fame for bringing suit in U.S. District Court that resulted in the ruling that segregation of Hispanic students was illegal.

Wrenn Junior High. This school is named after Elizabeth T. Wrenn, the district's first black teacher.

McFarlin Tennis Center. This first-class tennis facility in San Pedro Park was named after John McFarlin, a millionaire who supported the Trinity University intercollegiate tennis program and helped them to achieve national prominence.

Bowen's Island. This small island in the San Antonio River, located across from the City Public Service Building, was named after its former owner, John Bowen, the city's first postmaster. At one time the island was six acres long, bounded by the river on three sides, and the Concepción Acequia on the other. Bowen bought the island in 1845 from Josefa Rodriguez de Yturri for $300 and built a seven-room house there. Bowen was a staunch Unionist, and his family claims that he hid fugitive slaves at his home. After his death in 1867, Bowen was buried on the island. In 1869 the acequia was filled in to make the island more of a peninsula. Throughout the years, the island has had many owners, including Daniel Boone. In 1870 it had a private garden, and the San Antonio chapter of the German athletic club Turn Verein was based there. The island became a popular gathering spot and a center for social activities. With the rerouting of the river, the island eventually shrank to its present minuscule size. The Tower Life Building, Granada Homes, and City Public Service Building sit on land that was originally Bowen's Island.

Witte Museum. Alfred G. Witte left the city $65,000 in his will to construct a museum in Brackenridge Park. It opened in October 1926.

McNay Art Museum. Originally a mansion owned by Marion Koogler McNay, the home was donated with the express purpose of becoming a museum.

Tobin Center for the Performing Arts. The charitable Tobin Endowment donated $15 million as a challenge grant to redevelop the old Municipal Auditorium into a new performing arts center.

Ewing Halsell pedestrian bridge. This bridge over the San Antonio River near the Museum of Art was a gift from Mark Watson, who saved it from the old Lone Star Brewery. A grant from the Ewing Halsell Foundation paid for its installation.

Nix Medical Center. This downtown medical landmark is named after J. M. Nix, the builder who constructed South Texas's first major medical complex in November 1930. Nix also built the Majestic Building, among other downtown properties.

Book Building. This recently renovated historic building is named after Dana Book, a civil engineer, who raised the office structure in 1906. Book came from New York City, where he was instrumental in the construction of that city's subway system.

Club Giraud. This private club on the grounds of the Southwest School of Art is named after François Giraud, the architect who designed the buildings for their original use, the old Ursuline convent.

FIRSTS

Historical

First city to desegregate. San Antonio was the first city in Texas to desegregate its schools and city facilities in 1954, with the lobbying efforts of city councilman Henry B. González. It was also one of the earliest cities in the South to open the doors to all.

First showing of *The Alamo*. The premiere of *The Alamo*, starring John Wayne, took place at the Woodlawn Theatre on Fredericksburg Road.

First movie about the Alamo. *The Immortal Alamo*, an American silent film produced by the Star Film Company and directed by French filmmaker Gaston Méliès, was released in 1911. The film, said to be ten minutes long, included extras from the nearby Peacock Military Academy.

First Fiesta event. The Battle of Flowers Parade is the oldest Fiesta event, a tradition which started in 1891. Although it was scheduled for April 21, rain postponed it until April 24.

First NIOSA. Patterned after early San Antonio fiestas, the first Night in Old San Antonio was a one-day event held in 1938. Originally called the Indian Festival, it was renamed the River Carnival in 1946 after taking a break during World War II. It became a Night in Old San Antonio in 1948, when the city asked the Conservation Society, who sponsored it, to move the event to Fiesta Week. In 1954 the event added a second day, and in 1958 it expanded to four days.

Innovations

First air mail. Marjorie Stinson flew the first air mail route in Texas on February 6, 1928, delivering mail between the municipalities of San Antonio and Seguin, covering a grand total of thirty miles.

First elevator. The Kampmann Building, constructed in 1883, was the city's first four-story building and also the first one to be equipped with an elevator.

First air-conditioned skyscraper. The Milam Building, at the corner of Soledad and Travis downtown, was not only the city's first totally air-conditioned skyscraper, but also the nation's tallest building. When it opened in 1928, San Antonians could not comprehend how air-conditioning would change the South.

First hotel with air-conditioning. The St. Anthony, a landmark hotel, has sat across from Travis Park since 1909, playing host to presidents and celebrities. Responsible for many innovations in the hotel industry, it was the first hotel in the world with air-conditioning, the first to have automatic doors, and the first to offer a drive-in registration desk.

First first-class hotel. The Menger Hotel opened on February 2, 1859, in its present location on Alamo Plaza. William Menger operated a brewery and opened the hotel to serve his patrons. The original building has been added on to several times.

Media

First newspaper. In 1849 the *Western Texian* was printed here, becoming the city's first newspaper.

First telegraph. Telegraph arrived in the city in 1876. It was used primarily to connect San Antonio with other military centers.

First telephone. The first telephone in San Antonio was installed on March 22, 1878, from the waterworks to the mayor's office, only four days after the first phone in Texas had been installed in

Galveston. However, a *San Antonio Express* article from June 11, 1893, states that Brackenridge had constructed a telephone line between his home and his downtown bank twenty years earlier, which would have made his the first phone line in the country. The article notes that other cities regarded Brackenridge's telephone as a fad.

First Academy Award–winning film. The first film ever to win the Oscar for Best Picture was *Wings,* which was filmed in San Antonio and premiered at the Texas Theatre on May 19, 1927.

First radio station. WOAI-AM was the city's first radio station, signing on with 500 watts on September 25, 1922. KTSA debuted on February 19, 1928, broadcasting from the Plaza Hotel (now the Granada Homes). KABC signed on later that year on December 1 from the Majestic Building, followed shortly by KONO radio, which had its programming originate from the Bluebonnet Hotel.

First television station. WOAI-TV Channel 4 was San Antonio's first television station, which went on the air on December 11, 1949, when there were approximately twenty-five TV sets in existence in the city. Originally it broadcast from 11 a.m. to 10:15 p.m. The station changed its call letters to KMOL in 1975 but is still located at 1031 Navarro Street. It was the first station to run Hollywood movies and to broadcast a church service. A CBS station, KENS, signed on in 1950, and an ABC station, KONO-TV (later KSAT), hit the airwaves in 1957.

First television newscaster. In the early days of WOAI-TV, the ten o'clock news was simulcast with WOAI Radio. Henry Guerra, Frank Mathews, and Jim Metcalf were the city's first anchors. Guerra was also heard for many years on WOAI radio. Few people know that besides being a pioneer broadcaster, Guerra is also an undertaker. Phil Hemphill was San Antonio's first television weatherman. In the mid-1960s Martha Buchanan became WOAI-TV's first on-camera newswoman and the state's first female anchor.

People

First fire department. San Antonio's first fire department was a volunteer group formed with German acrobats from the Turn Verein.

First nonmilitary or religious settlers. In March 1731, fifty-six men, women, and children from the Canary Islands arrived in San Antonio by royal edict from Spain. Previously, the area was occupied mainly by missionaries and soldiers. It took one year for the pioneers to travel from the coast of Africa to Mexico, then across land to San Antonio.

First symphony. The first symphony orchestra in Texas was formed in San Antonio in 1887.

First Hispanic city councilman. Henry B. González was San Antonio's first Hispanic city councilman (1953), the first Mexican American elected to the state senate (1956), and the first Hispanic elected to the U.S. House of Representatives (1961).

First Hispanic mayor of the modern era. Elected in 1981, Henry Cisneros became the city's first Mexican American mayor since the early nineteenth century and the first Hispanic to lead a city the size of San Antonio.

First woman mayor. Lila Cockrell was the first female mayor in San Antonio's history. She was elected twice, the term before Henry Cisneros and the term after.

First women soldiers. The First Company of the Women's Army Auxiliary Corps was stationed at Fort Sam Houston in 1942. A plaque at the site where their barracks once stood honors these military pioneers.

First service clubs. The Rotary Club first organized in San Antonio in June 1912, with ten members and Herbert J. Hays as president. The Lions Club was formed locally on January 17, 1919, with twenty-one members and William L. Stiles as its president.

Places

First boarding school for girls. Established in 1851, Ursuline Academy was the first boarding school for girls in San Antonio and the second in Texas.

First public secondary school. San Antonio High School opened on Main Avenue in 1879 as the city's first public high school. In 1917, when Brackenridge High School opened, San Antonio High School became Main Avenue High School. Fox Tech High School now occupies that site.

First public junior college. San Antonio College was the first public junior college in Texas, opening in 1925 and occupying the old German-English School on S. Alamo. The college moved to its present location on San Pedro in 1951.

First Chinese school. The state's first Chinese school was established in San Antonio in 1922 and was located at 215 San Saba Street.

First Chinese Baptist church. The church, on Avenue B near the Valero Building, was the first of its kind in the South and opened its doors in 1923.

First Catholic church. Mission San Antonio de Valero was founded on May 1, 1718, about two miles south of San Pedro Springs. The mission, known today as the Alamo, moved to its present site in 1724.

First Episcopal church. The cornerstone for St. Mark's Episcopal Church was laid in 1859, but construction was halted in 1861 because of the Civil War. The half-completed structure was often mistaken for an old mission. Finally completed in 1874, it was the city's first Episcopal church. Lieutenant Colonel Robert E. Lee, who was stationed in San Antonio in the mid-1800s, was an early member of its congregation. The bell for the church was cast in Troy, New York, with metal from a cannon used at the Alamo. It is located next to Travis Park.

First Jewish congregation. The Temple Beth-El was the city's first synagogue. Its first temple was located near Travis Park and constructed in 1875. Its present site near San Antonio College was built in 1927.

First park. In 1729 Philip V of Spain, via his viceroy in Mexico, declared the grounds at the headwaters of the springs an *ejido,* or public land, making San Pedro Park the oldest park in San Antonio. Travis Park was the second park in the city.

First public housing project. The Alazán-Apache Courts on the city's west side was not only the first of its kind in San Antonio but one of the first public housing projects in the nation.

First museum. The city's first museum, a museum of natural history, was built in 1885 in San Pedro Park.

First oil production. A plaque on SE Military Drive near Goliad Road commemorates the first productive oil well in Texas. Near the present site of Brooks AFB, forty-nine barrels of black gold were pumped in 1889 on George Dullnig's ranch.

First for-profit hospital. The Nix Hospital opened in November 1930 at its present location downtown, marking a new era in hospital care. The twenty-four-story structure had the distinction of being the only building in America that housed a hospital, doctors' offices, and a parking garage.

First two-story building. In 1780 Fray Pedro Fuentes built a two-story building on Flores Street, the first in San Antonio.

First brewery. William Menger opened the first brewery in the Alamo City in 1855, which was also the first brewery in Texas.

First national bank. George Brackenridge opened the San Antonio National Bank in 1866 at 239 E. Commerce in a building that is now occupied by lawyers' offices. Brackenridge lived in the adjacent building, and legend has it that the noted philanthropist kept a cow on the roof in order to guarantee a supply of fresh milk.

First Mexican restaurant. Located at 231 Losoya, the original Mexican restaurant was aptly named the Original Mexican Restaurant. Operated by the Farnsworth family, it opened in 1899; before that, Mexican food was sold mainly in open-air markets or in *fondas,* front rooms of the homes of former chili queens.

The restaurant closed in 1961 and reopened on the River Walk in the 1980s.

First drive-thru restaurant. The local Pig Stands claim to be the world's first restaurants to offer service to patrons seated in their automobiles.

First Luby's. Luby's Cafeterias started in the basement of a hotel on College and Presa Streets. That location is now occupied by the Bayous Restaurant.

First Sears store. The city's first outlet for this nationwide superstore opened on March 7, 1929, in the Smith-Young Tower (now the Tower Life Building).

First mall. North Star Mall, opening in 1960, was the city's first mall, with H-E-B and a Walgreens as its first tenants.

Sports

First city team to win a state championship. The 1926 Brackenridge Eagles men's basketball team, coached by D. C. "Bobby" Cannon, was the first city team to win a state title. The Eagles were undefeated until they lost to a team from Kansas City and ended up fourth in the national tourney. The team was unique because it played its home games on an outdoor hardwood court, believed to be the only one in the nation.

First San Antonio college team to win an NCAA championship. In 1972 the Tigers from Trinity University won the NCAA Tennis Championship.

First San Antonio college on "College GameDay." On September 13, 2014, the game between University of Incarnate Word and North Dakota State was the featured contest on ESPN's "College GameDay." UIW lost to NDSU 58–0 in a game played in Fargo, North Dakota.

First championship baseball team. The San Antonio entry in the Texas League won its pennant in 1897.

First radio broadcast of a local baseball game. In 1929 Earl Wilson of KTAP radio was the first to broadcast a local game.

Transportation

First road. The Camino Real, or King's Highway, was established by the Spanish and is believed to be the oldest road in America.

First railroad. February 16, 1877, was the date the first train rolled into town. The Galveston, Harrisburg, and San Antonio Railway chugged into the city on the newly created Sunset Line. The railway is now known as the Southern Pacific.

First streetcars. Mule-driven streetcars first appeared on the city's roadways in June 1878, taking visitors from downtown to San Pedro Park, which at that time was on the outskirts of the city. The first electric streetcars arrived in San Antonio in 1890.

First coast-to-coast paved road. The Old Spanish Trail was started in 1915 and completed in 1924. It passed through San Antonio and was the first paved road to connect the Atlantic to the Pacific.

First airplane flight. Lieutenant Benjamin Delahauf Foulois of the U.S. Army was the first to become airborne in San Antonio. On March 2, 1910, at 9:30 a.m., the young army pilot catapulted his Wright Brothers Flyer above the Arthur MacArthur parade ground on Fort Sam Houston, not only beginning the era of military flight, but also giving birth to what eventually became the U.S. Air Force.

First airport. Early flights in San Antonio took off from the parade ground at Fort Sam Houston. In 1915, after an appeal by aviatrix Marjorie Stinson, the city opened Stinson Field on the city's southwest side. The field is still in use and is one of the three oldest airports in the nation.

ACKNOWLEDGMENTS

The number one question I was asked when I wrote my first novel, *The Travis Club*, was, Are all these tales of San Antonio's history in the book true? I would respond with an enthusiastic yes, and a second question would inevitably follow: Where can I get your other book, *San Antonio Uncovered*?

The Texas publisher who brought the book to the shelves in 1992 had been bought by a larger house, which let the book go out of print. I had pretty much lost hope that *San Antonio Uncovered* would be printed again.

Then in 2014, out of the blue, Tom Payton from Trinity University Press contacted me, expressing interest in an updated edition of the book. I am profoundly grateful to him, as without him, this book would have passed into obscurity. I also owe a huge debt of gratitude to Steffanie Mortis at the press for guiding me through the process of revising a twenty-year-old book.

Thank you to Chris Hall, Amy Stone, and Jennifer Mathews for your time and your stories. Special thanks to Bill Manchester from the Fort Sam Houston Museum, who was an invaluable resource on local military history.

Thanks to George Dawson, a docent at the San Antonio Missions National Park. He spent ten years researching a local legend and rediscovered the phenomena of solar illuminations. Thank you, Bob "Daddy-O" Wade, for our long afternoon interview. Readers are probably familiar with his giant boots on Loop 410. His story and his spirit are Texas treasures. Thank you, Paul Anderson and Workhouse Media, for your continued support and assistance.

Special thanks to the San Antonio Convention and Visitors Bureau, the *San Antonio Express-News*, the San Antonio Public Library, and all the other San Antonians who kept a copy of the original book and let me know how much they still refer to it. An incredible number of people contributed to the earlier editions of the book. I will never forget your help over the three years it took to research and write them.

Finally, a loving and heartfelt thank-you to my wife and my best friend, Madelyn, who for some reason was attracted to my sense of curiosity and has always encouraged me to follow my dreams. I am finished; it is time to come out of my back office and rejoin our family.

INDEX

An award-winning disc jockey, Mark Louis Rybczyk started his career at KXZL, WOAI, and KJ-97 in San Antonio before moving to FM 96.3 KSCS in Dallas, where he has the longest-running morning show in the Dallas–Fort Worth area. Rybczyk also penned *The Travis Club*, a historical thriller based on San Antonio lore.